Hypochondriasis and Health Anxiety

About the Authors

Jonathan S. Abramowitz, PhD, is Associate Chair of Psychology and Professor and Director of the Anxiety and Stress Disorders Clinic at the University of North Carolina at Chapel Hill. He has authored or edited ten books and over 100 research articles and book chapters on anxiety and related disorders. He serves as Associate Editor of two professional journals: *Behavior Research and Therapy* and the *Journal of Cognitive Psychotherapy*.

Autumn E. Braddock, PhD, is a clinical health psychologist within the Veterans Affairs Greater Los Angeles Healthcare System, specializing in behavioral medicine and cognitive-behavioral therapy for anxiety disorders. She has multiple publications and has presented her research, primarily addressing anxiety within medical populations, at national and international conferences.

Advances in Psychotherapy – Evidence-Based Practice

Danny Wedding; PhD, MPH, Prof., St. Louis, MO
(Series Editor)
Larry Beutler; PhD, Prof., Palo Alto, CA
Kenneth E. Freedland; PhD, Prof., St. Louis, MO
Linda C. Sobell; PhD, ABPP, Prof., Ft. Lauderdale, FL
David A. Wolfe; PhD, Prof., Toronto
(Associate Editors)

The basic objective of this series is to provide therapists with practical, evidence-based treatment guidance for the most common disorders seen in clinical practice – and to do so in a "reader-friendly" manner. Each book in the series is both a compact "how-to-do" reference on a particular disorder for use by professional clinicians in their daily work, as well as an ideal educational resource for students and for practice-oriented continuing education.

The most important feature of the books is that they are practical and "reader-friendly:" All are structured similarly and all provide a compact and easy-to-follow guide to all aspects that are relevant in real-life practice. Tables, boxed clinical "pearls", marginal notes, and summary boxes assist orientation, while checklists provide tools for use in daily practice.

Hypochondriasis and Health Anxiety

Jonathan S. Abramowitz
University of North Carolina at Chapel Hill, NC

Autumn E. Braddock
Veterans Affairs of Greater Los Angeles Healthcare System, CA

HOGREFE

Library of Congress Cataloging in Publication

is available via the Library of Congress Marc Database under the
LC Control Number 2010933424

Library and Archives Canada Cataloguing in Publication

Abramowitz, Jonathan S.
        Hypochondriasis and health anxiety / Jonathan S. Abramowitz, Autumn E.
Braddock. -- 1st ed.

(Advances in psychotherapy--evidence-based practice ; v. 19) Includes bibliographical references.
ISBN 978-0-88937-325-9

        1. Hypochondria. 2. Hypochondria--Treatment. 3. Anxiety--Treatment.
4. Cognitive therapy. I. Braddock, Autumn E II. Title. III. Series: Advances in psychotherapy--evidence-based
practice ; v.19

RC552.H8A27 2010   616.85'25   C2010-905200-5

PUBLISHING OFFICES
USA: Hogrefe Publishing, 875 Massachusetts Avenue, 7th Floor, Cambridge, MA 02139
                    Phone (866) 823-4726, Fax (617) 354-6875; E-mail customerservice@hogrefe-publishing.com
EUROPE: Hogrefe Publishing, Rohnsweg 25, 37085 Göttingen, Germany
                    Phone +49 551 49609-0, Fax +49 551 49609-88, E-mail publishing@hogrefe.com

SALES & DISTRIBUTION
USA: Hogrefe Publishing, Customer Services Department,
                    30 Amberwood Parkway, Ashland, OH 44805
                    Phone (800) 228-3749, Fax (419) 281-6883, E-mail customerservice@hogrefe.com
EUROPE: Hogrefe Publishing, Rohnsweg 25, 37085 Göttingen, Germany
                    Phone +49 551 49609-0, Fax +49 551 49609-88, E-mail publishing@hogrefe.com

OTHER OFFICES
CANADA: Hogrefe Publishing, 660 Eglinton Ave. East, Suite 119-514, Toronto, Ontario, M4G 2K2
SWITZERLAND: Hogrefe Publishing, Länggass-Strasse 76, CH-3000 Bern 9

Hogrefe Publishing
Incorporated and registered in the Commonwealth of Massachusetts, USA, and in Göttingen, Lower Saxony,
Germany

Printed and bound in the USA
ISBN: 978-0-88937-325-9

Dedication

To our respective families: Stacy, Emily, and Miriam; Eric, Alyxzandria, and Sienna. Your love puts everything in perspective.

Preface

This volume in the *Advances in Psychotherapy: Evidence-Based Practice* series describes the conceptualization, assessment, and psychological treatment of severe health anxiety, hypochondriasis, and related problems using empirically supported cognitive-behavioral therapy (CBT) techniques. The development of effective problem-focused treatments for severe health anxiety has created a growing need for the dissemination of treatment manuals, such as this one, to mental health professionals who want to know how to use these techniques with their patients.

This book builds upon psychological principles of behavior change. As such, it assumes that the reader has basic knowledge and some training in psychotherapeutic intervention. It is written for psychologists, psychiatrists, physicians, nurses, physician aides, social workers, students and trainees, and other health care practitioners who encounter patients with unexplained physical complaints.

The book is divided into five chapters. The first chapter describes the clinical phenomenon of health anxiety and related problems, and describes empirically supported diagnostic and assessment procedures. Chapter 2 reviews what is known about the leading theoretical models of health anxiety and their implications for successful treatment. In Chapter 3, we present a framework for conducting an initial assessment and for deciding whether a patient is a candidate for the psychological treatment program outlined in Chapter 4. Methods for discussing the psychological (as opposed to medical) aspects of treatment, and strategies for getting the patient to "buy in" to a psychological approach are also incorporated in Chapter 3. Chapter 4 presents the nuts and bolts of psychological treatment techniques for health anxiety. It also reviews scientific evidence for the efficacy of this program and describes a number of common obstacles to successful treatment. Finally, Chapter 5 includes a case example of the treatment of severe health anxiety. A variety of forms and patient handouts for use in treatment appear in the appendix.

Health anxiety is a heterogeneous clinical condition. Some patients experience fears of dying a slow death due to cancer, while others have recurring, anxiety-evoking doubts that their unexplained pain or other bodily sensations are symptoms of a rare or previously undiscovered disease. At the time of this writing, the DSM-V Task Force on Somatoform Disorders is considering a new diagnosis, Complex Somatic Symptom Disorder, which would be even more heterogeneous and subsume a number of DSM-IV-TR conditions, such as hypochondriasis, somatization disorder, pain disorders, and undifferentiated somatoform disorder.

Although a systematic and multicomponent treatment approach is advocated in this book, we do not intend it to be a "cookbook." Rather, it guides the clinician in tailoring specific treatment components to individual patients' needs. It provides a practical and structured approach with supporting didactic materials for both clinicians and patients.

Acknowledgments

We are indebted to many people, including series editor Danny Wedding, associate editor Ken Freedland, and Robert Dimbleby of Hogrefe Publishing, for their invaluable guidance and suggestions. We also appreciate Kristy Gura's hard work in helping us prepare this book for publication. The pages of this volume echo clinical insights we acquired during our work at the Mayo Clinic in Rochester, Minnesota. We are grateful for the support of terrific colleagues including Stephen Whiteside, Sarah Kalsy, Brett Deacon, Katherine Moore, Kristi Dahlman, and Jill Snuggerud.

Dr. Braddock acknowledges the professional mentorship of Gary Wolfe, PhD, and Lisa Altman, MD, who have given unwavering support of primary care psychology and patient-centered care within the VA of Greater Los Angeles Healthcare System. She also thanks her colleagues Kellie Condon, PhD; Leigh Anne Selby, PsyD; and Mike Young, LCSW, and the numerous primary care providers, for their ongoing collaboration, guidance, and friendship.

Jointly, we dedicate this book to the brave patients who came to us – sometimes unwillingly – when their search for a medical explanation for their bodily complaints turned up empty. Not knowing what to expect, they courageously challenged themselves to embrace a psychological perspective on their complaints. They accepted their bodily sensations as benign, confronted their fears, and defeated their anxiety. They believed in us, confided in us, challenged us, and educated us. We thank them for their willingness to open their minds to our approach.

Table of Contents

1   Description of Health Anxiety

2   Theories and Models of Health Anxiety

3   Diagnosis and Treatment Indications

1

Description of Health Anxiety

1.1   Terminology

Anxiety is a cognitive, emotional, physiological, and behavioral response to the perception of threat. It occurs when one doubts his or her ability to cope with the perceived threat. **Health anxiety** refers to inappropriate or excessive health-related fears based on misperceptions of innocuous bodily cues and sensations as indicative of a serious medical problem. Moreover, the individual with health anxiety perceives him or herself as unable to cope with or prevent the perceived threat, in this case the presence of a serious medical illness.

1.2   Definition

Anxiety is an adaptive response which prepares us to take action when confronted with possible danger (i.e., the *fight or flight* response). Some degree of health-related anxiety may therefore be constructive if it motivates a person to take appropriate measures or seek proper medical attention. For example, apprehension concerning shortness of breath in a person with asthma can lead to prompt administration of inhalant bronchodilator medication to prevent respiratory fatigue or even death by suffocation. **Clinical health anxiety**, on the other hand, is extreme in relation to the actual degree of threat (if any threat even exists). It causes distress and interferes with various domains of functioning, including interpersonal relationships, self-care, work or school, and leisure.

Definition of health anxiety and hypochondriasis

Hypochondriasis. Hypochondriasis is classified as a somatoform disorder in DSM-IV-TR (American Psychiatric Association [APA], 2000) and characterized by a preoccupation with fears of having, or the idea that one has, a serious medical condition such as a chronic, life threatening or life-altering sickness (see Table 1). This "disease conviction" is (a) based on a misinterpretation of harmless or minor bodily sensations or perturbations and (b) persists in spite of appropriate medical evaluation and reassurance of good health.

The health-related preoccupation might concern specific bodily functions such as peristalsis or heart beat; slight benign abnormalities, signs, and sensations such as an occasional cough, pulled muscle, mole, or bruise on the skin; vague and ambiguous complaints such as "a hollow head" or "weak spine;" or specific organs (e.g., kidneys), body parts (e.g., prostate gland), or diseases (e.g., rabies, cancer).

Table 1
Summary of the DSM-IV-TR Diagnostic Criteria for Hypochondriasis

A. Preoccupation with fears of having, or the idea that one has, a serious disease based on the person's misinterpretation of bodily symptoms.

B. The preoccupation persists despite appropriate medical evaluation and reassurance.

C. The belief in criterion A is not a delusion and is not restricted to a circumscribed concern about appearance (as in Body Dysmorphic Disorder).

D. The preoccupation causes clinically significant distress or impairment in social, occupational, or other important areas of functioning.

E. The duration of the disturbance is at least 6 months.

F. The preoccupation is not better accounted for by another Axis I disorder such as Generalized Anxiety Disorder, Obsessive-Compulsive Disorder, Panic Disorder, a Major Depressive Episode, Separation Anxiety, or another Somatoform Disorder.

Adapted from the DSM-IV diagnostic criteria for hypochondriasis (American Psychiatric Association [APA], 1994). Adapted with permission.

Patients with clinical health anxiety often fixate on the cause, meaning, and authenticity of their complaints. Common expressions of this fixation include excessive seeking of reassurance about the physical complaints (e.g., repeated doctor visits and unnecessary tests), asking questions of medical professionals, seeking information from medical texts and websites, and extensive body checking (e.g., inspecting the skin, inspecting excrement, repeatedly measuring vital signs). Some patients avoid external triggers of health anxiety (e.g., hospitals, people with illnesses). Table 2 lists some common hypochondriacal and health anxiety-related behaviors.

Clinical Pearl
Hypochondriasis Versus Health Anxiety

The term "health anxiety" is beginning to replace the term "hypochondriasis" for the following reasons:

1. "Health anxiety" provides a clearer and more meaningful description of the emotional and behavioral aspects of this problem. "Hypochondriasis," on the other hand, derives from the Greek hypo (below) and chondros (cartilage of the breast bone) and was used by ancient Greek physicians to describe unexplained stomach pains. During the 19th Century, this became the male counterpart to hysteria.

2. Hypochondriasis is but one of several clinical disorders that involve health-related fears and worries. Thus, health anxiety is not a clinical diagnosis per se, but rather a phenomenon that can be present in a number of psychological conditions as well as medical diagnoses that often present with overlapping psychological symptoms (as we describe below).

3. Whereas the term "health anxiety" is more or less value neutral, "hypochondriasis" has pejorative connotations.

Table 2
Examples of Common Hypochondriacal and Health Anxiety-Related Behaviors

Checking and assurance-seeking
- Repeated visits to doctors to have symptoms checked
- "Doctor-shopping" to check if the diagnosis is correct
- Repeated Internet searches to find information about a certain symptom
- Repeatedly discussing or asking questions about the feared problem
- Reviewing test results and notes taken during doctor visits
- Persistently mentioning and describing symptoms to others
- Repeatedly reviewing medical texts or journal articles for information about illnesses or body symptoms

Body checking
- Repeatedly measuring heart rate, blood pressure, temperature, etc.
- Constantly monitoring levels of "throat tightness," dizziness, or pain
- Frequently palpating the throat or breasts for lumps
- Checking urine and stool for blood and consistency
- Frequent inspections of sores and moles on the skin

Safety signals
- Remain within a certain distance of the doctor's office, hospital, or medical center
- Keep medications on hand at all times
- Swallowing until it feels "normal"
- Rigid adherence to a strict diet

Avoidance
- Hospitals
- People with illnesses
- Television shows, movies, news articles, and other stories about sick people, illnesses, or death
- Physical exertion
- Routine physical exams
- Self-examinations (e.g., breast, testicles)
- Funerals and cemeteries

Poor Insight. Some individuals with hypochondriasis recognize that their health-related fears, preoccupations, and behaviors are excessive (i.e., they have "good insight"). The DSM-IV-TR diagnostic specifier, "**with poor insight**" is reserved for those who, most of the time, do not realize that their health-related fears and concerns are unrealistic.

Patients vary in terms of their insight into the excessiveness of their health concerns

1.3 Epidemiology

The lifetime prevalence of hypochondriasis in the general population has been estimated at anywhere between 0.02% and 7.7%. In primary care settings, estimates range from 0.8% to 8.5%. The estimated prevalence is 1.2% among cardiology outpatients and 1.0% among chronic pain patients. Men and women are about equally likely to be affected (APA, 2000).

1.4   Course and Prognosis

Most patients with health anxiety require professional help to avoid long-term suffering

Although symptoms of health anxiety may be present at any age, little is known about the average age of onset, or about the prevalence of health anxiety among children. Onset usually occurs in early adulthood, which coincides with the time at which most people assume greater responsibility for maintaining personal health. Other potential onset triggers include increased life stress, a personal experience with illness, the illness or death of a loved one, and exposure to mass media coverage of illnesses. Some health anxiety patients endure a long-term burden of functional impairment and personal distress if effective treatment is not sought.

1.5   Differential Diagnoses

A number of psychological disorders involve health anxiety to one degree or another

Health anxiety is not a DSM-IV-TR diagnosis. Rather, it is a collection of signs and symptoms featuring medically unexplained physical complaints; fears, concerns, and preoccupation with health and illness; and behaviors such as avoidance, checking, and other types of reassurance-seeking. Hypochondriasis can be

---

Table 3
Proposed Diagnostic Criteria for Complex Somatic Symptom Disorder (CSSD) in DSM-V

Criteria A, B, and C are necessary:

A. Somatic symptoms:

Multiple somatic symptoms that are distressing, or one severe symptom

B. Misattributions, excessive concern or preoccupation with symptoms and illness: At least two of the following are required to meet this criterion:
   1. *High level of health-related anxiety.*
   2. *Normal bodily symptoms are viewed as threatening and harmful*
   3. *A tendency to assume the worst about their health (catastrophizing).*
   4. *Belief in the medical seriousness of their symptoms despite evidence to the contrary.*
   5. *Health concerns assume a central role in their lives*

C. Chronicity: Although any one symptom may not be continuously present, the state of being symptomatic is chronic and persistent (at least 6 months).

The following optional specifiers may be applied to a diagnosis of CSSD where one of the following dominates the clinical presentation:
   1. Multiplicity of somatic complaints (somatization disorder in DSM-IV)
   2. High health anxiety (hypochondriasis in DSM-IV) [If patients present solely with health-related anxiety in the absence of somatic symptoms, they may be more appropriately diagnosed as having an anxiety disorder.]
   3. Pain disorder. This classification is reserved for individuals presenting predominantly with pain complaints who also have many of the features described under criterion B. Patients with other presentations of pain may better fit other psychiatric diagnoses such as major depression or adjustment disorder.

considered the quintessential "health anxiety disorder," yet it is one of several conditions characterized by health anxiety. At the time of this writing, the DSM-V Task Force on Somatoform Disorders is considering a new diagnosis – **Complex Somatic Symptom Disorder (CSSD)** – to encompass many of the conditions described below. The diagnostic criteria for the proposed CSSD appear in Table 3.

1.5.1   Somatization Disorder

Somatization disorder is defined in DSM-IV-TR as involving a persistent pattern of chronic, medically unexplained physical complaints beginning before age 30. The focus of the physical complaints may shift over time, but the complaints always result in excessive treatment-seeking and substantial impairment in social, occupational, or other areas of functioning. To meet criteria for this condition, the individual must experience pain (e.g., headache), gastrointestinal symptoms (e.g., unexplained vomiting), problems with sexual functioning (e.g., dysparunia), or at least one pseudoneurological symptom (e.g., chronic dizziness) . Repeated doctor visits and "shopping around" for new doctors are common. Patients frequently feel disparaged and misunderstood when medical tests repeatedly come up negative.

1.5.2   Somatic Delusions

Somatic delusions (included in the DSM-IV-TR under Delusional Disorder, Somatic Type) involve bizarre, fixed beliefs about one's health. For example, the belief that one is emitting a foul odor, infested with insects or parasites, or that certain parts of the body (contrary to objective observation) are misshapen or not functioning properly. These patients might seek medical attention or take additional measures for their supposed condition (e.g., contacting pest control agencies to exterminate supposed infestation). It is unclear whether somatic delusions are best considered symptoms of hypochondriasis with poor insight, or whether they are indeed psychotic symptoms.

1.5.3   Illness or Disease Phobia

Illness phobia (or disease phobia) is described in the DSM-IV-TR as a specific phobia and is defined as an unreasonable fear of contracting a disease. Core features include distress, apprehension, and avoidance of situations that are perceived to lead to the feared illness. Whereas illness phobia involves fear of *developing* a disease (through means other than contamination as in obsessive-compulsive disorder, hypochondriasis involves the conviction that the feared disease is *already present*. Moreover, whereas hypochondriasis is characterized by somatic complaints, such complaints are not always present in illness phobia. Finally, illness phobia typically involves fears of acutely life-threatening conditions (e.g., choking, heart attack, stroke), whereas the feared health consequences in hypochondriasis are typically long-term and progressive (e.g., slow physical or mental decline).

1.5.4   Panic Disorder

Panic disorder is an anxiety disorder in DSM-IV-TR involving recurrent, unexpected panic attacks that involve intense physiological (anxious) arousal (e.g., rapid heart rate, shortness of breath, dizziness, tingling sensations), as well as a subjective sense of doom and fear (e.g., "I'm dying," "I'm having a heart attack," etc.) and behavioral avoidance of situations that might trigger an attack (APA, 2000). Many patients with panic disorder attribute these sensations to organic causes (e.g., a heart attack) and may seek excessive medical examination, avoid sources of bodily stress (e.g., strenuous activity), and engage in behaviors that lead them to feel safe from panic or a medical emergency (e.g., keeping medication or a cell phone on-hand at all times).

Although many people with hypochondriasis also have panic attacks, patients with panic disorder experience a sense of doom during panic attacks that involves fears of *immediate* and life-threatening physical catastrophe (e.g., a heart attack, aneurysm). In hypochondriasis, patients display a more insipid fear of *delayed* or protracted consequences (e.g., "I am slowly dying from lung cancer and no doctor will help me").

1.5.5   Obsessive-Compulsive Disorder

Obsessive-compulsive disorder (OCD), also an anxiety disorder, is characterized by (a) recurrent intrusive senseless thoughts, ideas, or images (obsessions) that provoke anxiety; and (b) efforts to resist obsessional anxiety by ritualistically engaging in some other thought or action (compulsive rituals; APA, 2000). Common obsessions include fears of making mistakes, unwanted sexual, violent or sacrilegious images, ideas of causing harm or bad luck, thoughts that objects are not arranged "just right," and thoughts of contamination and illnesses. Common compulsive rituals include washing and cleaning, checking, repeating routine behaviors (e.g., repeatedly turning off the light switch), re-ordering, counting, seeking reassurance, and mentally replacing unacceptable thoughts with "good" or "safe" thoughts.

Some authors have likened the persistent preoccupation with illness in hypochondriasis and other forms of health anxiety to obsessions in OCD, whereas the repetitive reassurance-seeking and checking with doctors are compulsive rituals (e.g., Fallon, Javitch, Hollander, & Liebowitz, 1991). While individuals with OCD tend to show multiple types of obsessions and compulsions, some of which may be concerned with health and illness, patients with hypochondriasis tend to be singly "obsessed" with health/illness-related concerns.

1.5.6   Generalized Anxiety Disorder

Persistent and uncontrollable doubt and worry, which are main features of generalized anxiety disorder (GAD), are also present in health anxiety. Individuals with GAD worry excessively about numerous mundane circumstances (e.g., relationships, work or school, finances, their own and others' health, and world affairs; APA, 2000). However, health-related worries in GAD are less frequent and less intrusive than those observed in hypochondriasis and health anxiety. Additionally, people with GAD report fewer somatic symptoms and fewer misinterpretations of specific bodily sensations relative to those with hypochondriasis.

1.5.7   Pain Disorder

The predominant feature of pain disorder, which is classified in the DSM-IV-TR (APA, 2000) as a somatoform disorder, is the perception of severe pain at one or more anatomic sites. The pain may or may not occur along with a medical condition, but it is not explained by organic factors and is reported as more severe than would typically be observed in patients with a medical condition. Individuals with health anxiety may report excessive pain, but they tend to perseverate on their fear that the symptoms are indicative of a serious medical illness.

1.6   Comorbidity

Comorbidity with other Axis I disorders is common. The most frequently co-occurring diagnoses are anxiety disorders, such as panic disorder and GAD. Unipolar mood disorders (e.g., depression and dysthymia) are also common. Estimates of the number of patients with comorbid conditions vary widely (e.g., from 20% to 70%).

Many people with health anxiety also suffer from other Axis I and Axis II psychological disorders

  Personality disorders (PDs) and personality traits characteristic of the anxious cluster (Cluster C; e.g., dependent), dramatic, emotional and erratic cluster (Cluster B; e.g., histrionic) and less often, the odd and eccentric cluster (Cluster A; schizotypal) may also co-occur with health anxiety and hypochondriasis. Prevalence rates vary widely from study to study.

1.7   Diagnostic Procedures and Documentation

This section reviews empirically established, structured and semi-structured diagnostic interviews, self-report measures, and methods for documenting symptom changes during a course of psychological treatment.

1.7.1   Structured Diagnostic Interviews

Two anxiety-focused structured interviews can be used to assess health anxiety symptoms: the **Anxiety Disorders Interview Schedule for DSM-IV** (ADIS; Brown, DiNardo, & Barlow, 1994) and the **Structured Diagnostic Interview for Hypochondriasis** (SDI-H; Barsky et al., 1992). The ADIS is available from Oxford University Press and the SDI-H can be found in Barsky and colleagues (1992). Additional structured interviews include the

Structured Clinical Interview for DSM-IV-TR (SCID-IV; First, Spitzer, Gibbon, & Williams, 1996) and the **Mini International Neuropsychiatric Interview** (MINI; Sheehan et al., 1998). The SCID-IV is available at www.scid4.org, and the MINI is available at no cost from https://www.medical-outcomes.com/HTMLFiles/MINI/MINI_Registration.htm. The MINI is preferable to the SCID due to its brevity and excellent reliability and validity. A limitation of some of these interviews, however, is that they do not contain a sufficient number of items assessing somatoform disorders. Thus, these tools may be best suited for ruling out co-occurring anxiety and mood disorders.

1.7.2   Semi-Structured Symptom Interviews

The Y-BOCS can be used to measure health anxiety symptoms

Although developed to measure OCD symptom severity, the Yale-Brown Obsessive Compulsive Scale (Y-BOCS; Goodman, Price, Rasmussen, Mazure, Delgado, et al., 1989; Goodman, Price, Rasmussen, Mazure, Fleischmann, et al., 1989) is a semi-structured interview that can also serve as a measure of health anxiety severity. The Y-BOCS includes 10 items to assess the following five parameters of obsessions (items 1-5) and compulsions (items 6-10): (a) time, (b) interference, (c) distress, (d) efforts to resist, and (e) perceived control. Each item is rated on a scale from 0-4 and the item scores are summed to produce a total score ranging from 0 (no symptoms) to 40 (extreme). When used to assess health anxiety, preoccupation with illness is scored on the obsessions subscale. Behaviors such as checking, reassurance-seeking, and consulting with doctors are scored on the compulsions subscale. Scores on each of the 10 items are summed to produce a total score ranging from 0 to 40. In most instances, scores of 0 to 7 represent subclinical symptoms, those from 8 to 15 represent mild symptoms, scores of 16 to 23 relate to moderate symptoms, scores from 24 to 31 suggest severe symptoms, and scores of 32 to 40 imply extreme symptoms. Our adapted version of this measure appears in Appendix A of our comprehensive text on the treatment of health anxiety (Abramowitz & Braddock, 2008). The reliability and validity of the Y-BOCS when used in this way, however, has not been formerly examined. As a measure of OCD, it is reliable, valid, and sensitive to the effects of treatment (Goodman, Price, Rasmussen, Mazure, Delgado, et al., 1989; Goodman, Price, Rasmussen, Mazure, Fleischmann, et al., 1989).

The BABS – a measure of insight in health anxiety

The **Brown Assessment of Beliefs Scale** (BABS; Eisen et al., 1998) is a brief, (7 items) continuous measure of insight into the senselessness of strongly held beliefs (e.g., beliefs about the presence of a serious illness), which has good reliability, validity, and sensitivity to change. Administration begins with the interviewer and patient identifying one or two of the patient's specific illness beliefs that have been of significant concern over the past week. Examples include, "My heart is weak and is likely to fail" and "The floaters in my eye indicate that I have a serious medical condition." Next, individual items assess the patient's (a) conviction in this belief, (b) perceptions of how others view this belief, (c) explanation for why others hold a different view, (d) willingness to challenge the belief, (e) attempts to disprove the belief, (f) insight into the senselessness of the belief, and (g) ideas/delusions of reference. Only the first six items are summed to produce a total score. The BABS is included in Appendix B of Abramowitz and Braddock (2008).

1.7.3 Self-Report Inventories

The **Short Health Anxiety Inventory** (SHAI; Salkovskis, Rimes, Warwick, & Clark, 2002) is an 18-item questionnaire that assesses health anxiety independent of physical health status. For each item the respondent chooses from a series of four statements (ranging in severity from 0 [least severe] to 3 [most severe]) that best reflects his or her feelings over the past several months. Items address the following aspects of health anxiety: worry about health, awareness of bodily sensations and changes, and feared consequences of having an illness. The SHAI contains two factors: (a) the feared likelihood of becoming ill and (b) the feared negative consequences of becoming ill. The measure has good reliability and validity in clinical and nonclinical samples and can also be used to assess health anxiety within other psychological disorders (e.g., anxiety disorders). The full SHAI is reprinted in an article by Salkovskis and colleagues (2002).

Self-report inventories are used to gather additional severity data

The SHAI – a brief screening measure of health anxiety severity

The **Illness Attitudes Scale** (IAS; Kellner, 1986; 1987) is a 29-item questionnaire that measures (a) fear of illness/disease/pain/death, (b) symptoms' interference with lifestyle, (c) treatment experience, and (d) disease conviction (Hadjistavropoulos, Frombach, & Asmundson, 1999). Respondents are asked how often a list of thoughts and behaviors occur, with responses ranging from "never" to "most of the time". Overall, the measure has good reliability and validity. This scale is reproduced in Kellner (1987).

The **Cognitions about Body and Health Questionnaire** (CBHQ; Rief, Hiller, & Margraf, 1998) is a 31-item measure developed to help differentiate individuals with severe health anxiety from those with somatization disorder. It measures catastrophic interpretations of (a) bodily complaints, (b) autonomic sensations, (c) bodily weakness, (d) bodily complaints, and (e) health habits. Items assess agreement with catastrophic interpretations of bodily complaints and are rated on a 4-point scale ranging from "completely wrong" to "completely right." Overall, the psychometric properties of the CBHQ are adequate. The CBHQ is reprinted in an article by Rief and colleagues (1998).

The CBHQ – a measure of the cognitive basis of health anxiety

1.7.4 Documenting Changes in Symptom Levels

Continual assessment of health anxiety and related symptoms throughout the course of psychological treatment assists the clinician in evaluating treatment response. It is not enough to simply assume that "he seems to be less preoccupied," or "it looks like she has cut down on her reassurance-seeking," or even for the patient to report that he or she "feels better." Periodic re-assessment, using the aforementioned diagnostic tools and comparison with baseline symptom levels, should be conducted to objectively clarify whether and in which ways treatment has been helpful, and to identify problems that may require further treatment.

Assessing health anxiety throughout a course of treatment

2

Theories and Models of Health Anxiety

The biopsychosocial model of health anxiety

This chapter outlines a well-studied **biopsychosocial theory** of the development and maintenance of health anxiety. The treatment implications of this model are also discussed.

2.1 Development of Health Anxiety

How does one develop problems with severe health anxiety?

According to the biopsychosocial model, health anxiety arises from normal physiological, psychological, and environmental processes. When people acquire certain maladaptive beliefs about health and illness, they begin routinely misinterpreting benign bodily sensations as indicative of serious illness.

2.1.1 The Human Body Is "Noisy"

We all have "noisy bodies"

The biopsychosocial model of health anxiety begins with the reality that the human body is ever-changing, that it is receptive and responsive to a myriad of external and internal stimuli, and that it has many interrelated systems that constantly influence one another. We may occasionally notice this "body noise," especially if we "listen" carefully enough (e.g., stomach grumbling, a "pulled" muscle). People with health anxiety, however, habitually listen to their bodies and therefore become exquisitely sensitive to even very subtle bodily variations that most people would ignore or not even detect. It is this hypervigilance to the near steady stream of more or less benign body cues and sensations that sets the stage for health anxiety. Table 4 lists common sources of benign bodily sensations, perturbations, and variations that are frequently misinterpreted as signs of serious illness.

2.1.2 Beliefs and Interpretations Lead to Health Anxiety

How we interpret body sensations determines how health anxious we become

Following from Beck's (1976) cognitive model of emotion, health anxiety results when benign bodily sensations are *misinterpreted* as signs that a serious medical condition is present (e.g., "This pain in my groin means I have prostate cancer"). Once this happens, the innocuous bodily sensations (e.g., body noise) become the target of preoccupation (hypervigilance), and the person tries to avoid or reduce the perceived threat. This sequence is depicted in Figure 1.

Table 4
Sources of Benign Bodily Sensations and Cues

Source	Description
Homeostasis (the body's self-regulatory processes)	Different systems are activated and deactivated depending upon the body's needs. For example, the body must maintain a near constant temperature and oxygen level. Thus, healthy people invariably experience normal fluctuations in their heart rate, breathing rate, muscle tension, sweat gland activity, etc.
Diet	Changes in diet may cause odorous or discolored urine, changes in stool texture, and gastrointestinal discomfort, bloating, and mild hypoglycemia, which can cause sweating, tachycardia, and faintness.
Emotional and physiological arousal	Emotions such as anxiety, fear, worry, elation, excitement and anger are all accompanied by activation of the body's sympathetic nervous system and the release of adrenaline. This produces uncomfortable but benign body changes such as increased heart rate, breathing, muscle tension, pupil dilation, sweating, salivation, nausea, urinary urgency, dizziness, among other sensations. Moreover, physiologic arousal may lead to exhaustion and fatigue, blurred vision, numbness and tingling, feelings of choking or smothering, pain, trembling and twitching, hot or cold flashes, and dry mouth.
Benign medical conditions	Many benign or minor medical conditions can produce vague and diffuse bodily sensations. Examples include aerophagia, rumination syndrome, irritable bowel syndrome, postural, orthostatic tachycardia syndrome, vertigo, floaters, lipomas, hives, uticaria, nonepileptic seizures, and vasovagal syncope.

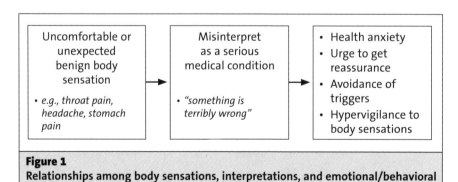

Figure 1
Relationships among body sensations, interpretations, and emotional/behavioral responses

Why do some people misappraise benign bodily sensations as threatening whereas others do not? Such misinterpretations result from dysfunctional core beliefs such as those summarized in Table 5.

Table 5
Domains of Dysfunctional Beliefs in Health Anxiety

Core belief	Description
Overestimates of threat	Beliefs that illnesses are more common, more easily transmitted, and more serious than they actually are
Anxiety sensitivity	Beliefs that the physical sensations associated with anxious arousal are dangerous
Intolerance of uncertainty	Belief that it is necessary (and possible) to be 100% certain that negative outcomes will not occur
Rigid health beliefs	Beliefs that being healthy requires being 100% symptom free and that all bodily signs and symptoms have a medical explanation
Maladaptive beliefs about general health	Belief that one is sick or especially susceptible to medical ailments
Distrust of medicine	Beliefs that physicians and medical tests are incompetent and invalid
Beliefs about death	Beliefs involving the assumption that consciousness endures after death

2.1.3   Origins of Dysfunctional Core Beliefs

Where do dysfunctional beliefs about body sensations come from?

Why do some people hold maladaptive, dysfunctional beliefs about health, illness, death, and medicine, such as those described in Table 5? Certain types of stressful or traumatic events, such as suffering from an illness or even watching a relative suffer, can lead a person to overestimate health risks. Many people with severe health anxiety report having had one or more bona fide medical problems in their past. Dysfunctional health-relevant beliefs might also be shaped by observing loved ones and authority figures deal with illnesses. Children, for example, learn attitudes about health and illness by watching their parents manage these situations. Overreactions to minor injuries, excessive use of healthcare, and frequent complaining could also convey to a child that *any* type of pain or injury is a *serious* problem that must not be ignored. Finally, health-related beliefs and attitudes may be transmitted directly through authority figures or via the media. Extensive media coverage of illnesses such as the H1N1 influenza epidemic in 2009, can also lead to overestimation of the probability, severity, and consequences of such conditions.

2.2   Maintenance of Health Anxiety

Why does health anxiety persist even if the person is medically healthy?

If clinical health anxiety develops from *mistaken* beliefs and *misinterpretations* of non-dangerous body sensations, why does it persist? Why don't people with this problem listen to their doctors, correct their flawed beliefs, and change their maladaptive behavior? Why do people with clinical health

Table 6
Summary of Maintenance Factors in Health Anxiety

Domain and Factor	Description
Physiological	
Fight-flight response	Harmless, anxiety-related bodily sensations seem like true medical problems, reaffirming the belief that one is ill.
Cognitive	
Selective attention to threat	Hypervigilance to normal "body noise" and other slight body sensations seems to confirm the presence of a feared illness.
Confirmation bias	Tendency to seek evidence that validates one's fear and discount information that invalidates the fear.
Memory bias	Tendency to inflate remembered estimates of the likelihood of illness.
Behavioral	
Safety behaviors and signals	Behaviors, stimuli, and situations associated with safety, which reduce anxiety in the short-term, but paradoxically prevent disconfirmation of illness fears.
Checking and reassurance-seeking	Excessive attempts to gain certainty of health status often lead to obtaining alarming information. Body checking may produce apparent "symptoms" of a feared disease.
Avoidance	Prevents disconfirmation of dysfunctional health beliefs.

anxiety fail to recognize that their fears and behaviors are inconsistent with the reassuring feedback they receive from medical professionals?

Several factors prevent such self-correction from occurring. These **maintenance factors** can be grouped into three domains: physiological, cognitive, and behavioral. The factors are summarized in Table 6 and discussed in detail next.

2.2.1 Physiological Maintenance Factors

When one becomes anxious or apprehensive about his or her health (or about any perceived threat, for that matter), the body's fight-flight mechanism is automatically activated, leading to bodily sensations (i.e., sympathetic arousal). These sensations may include a racing heartbeat, chest tightness, shortness of breath, fatigue, muscle tension, trembling, and gastrointestinal distress. This response might also involve blurred vision (or seeing spots), numbness or tingling in the extremities, hot or cold flashes, and sweating. A person who habitually misconstrues these benign sensations as additional evidence of illness may experience an escalation in health anxiety. That is, at the

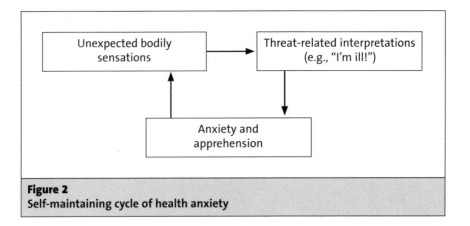

Figure 2
Self-maintaining cycle of health anxiety

very moment one becomes worried about his/her health, additional threatening "symptoms" emerge that seemingly confirm the presence of an illness. The result is a self-maintaining vicious cycle as outlined in Figure 2.

2.2.2 Cognitive Maintenance Factors

The presence of anxious apprehension affects cognitive processing in three ways which may maintain problems with health anxiety. These are described below.

Selective Attention to Threat Cues. It is adaptive to be vigilant about threat cues when danger is perceived; *not* paying attention to sources of harm could be deadly. Thus, anxious apprehension is naturally accompanied by an automatic shift in attention to the perceived threat. Even if the perceived threat is not objectively dangerous, such as in the case of benign bodily sensations in health anxiety, increased attention produces exquisite sensitivity to the feared stimulus. This may amplify vague and harmless bodily sensations and seem to confirm the belief that a serious illness is present.

Confirmation Bias. Additionally, it is adaptive to gather information when a potential threat is present. In the case of a perceived illness, one will seek information to validate (or invalidate) his or her concerns. When anxious, however, people tend to err on the side of caution (i.e., rely on *fear-confirming* information) since the costs of assuming good health when an illness is present are significantly higher than those associated with assuming illness when one is actually healthy. Yet in the case of health anxiety, reliance on danger-confirming information (while discounting danger-disconfirming evidence) maintains the faulty belief that a serious illness is present.

Confirmation bias can alter the impact of health information obtained from medical professionals, friends, relatives, the Internet, or other sources. For example, if a doctor orders an additional test "just to be sure," a health anxious individual might interpret this as evidence that an illness is present. Disconfirmatory evidence (e.g., numerous negative test results), on the other hand, may be dismissed as inadequate or immaterial. This phenomenon accounts for urges to seek second, third or even fourth opinions when doctors conclude that there is no sign of illness.

Memory Bias. Individuals with health anxiety appear to remember medical reports incorrectly and in ways which inflate estimates of the likelihood of illness as compared to what doctors actually tell them. Thus, even if doctors provide reassurance that a serious disease is unlikely, patients with health anxiety may remember this information in ways that exacerbate their fears.

2.2.3 Behavioral Maintenance Factors

When a threat is present, acting to ensure safety is adaptive. However, when there is no serious, objective threat, as in the case of health anxiety, such "safety behaviors" unintentionally maintain fear and anxiety. The types of safety behaviors commonly observed in health anxiety are described next.

The ways that health anxious people attempt to cope with their anxiety can make matters worse

Situational Safety Behaviors and Safety Signals. As described in Chapter 1 (Table 2), health anxious individuals use various strategies to make themselves feel safer and more certain about their health status. ***Safety behaviors*** are enacted to avert danger (e.g., calling a nurse to ask about a particular "symptom"). ***Safety signals*** are situations or stimuli the person associates with anxiety reduction. For example, using a blood pressure cuff to repeatedly check one's blood pressure is a *safety behavior*; the cuff itself is a *safety signal* if it is kept "just in case it is needed." These behaviors and signals, however, prevent the person from discovering that his or her health anxiety is unfounded. Put another way, following events which should verify that a feared illness is unlikely, health anxious individuals who habitually use safety behaviors and signals erroneously believe that the feared illness would have otherwise occurred had it not been for their own actions. Thus, the faulty illness beliefs are maintained.

Checking and Reassurance-Seeking. The most typical safety behavior in health anxiety is checking, which may include repeatedly querying medical professionals, family members, friends, the Internet, or textbooks, and closely inspecting one's own body. One way in which such behaviors maintain health anxiety is by increasing the likelihood of receiving a false positive (or ambiguous) result, which is misinterpreted as evidence for illness. Moreover, if slightly different (or seemingly contradictory) information is obtained from different sources, or on different occasions from the same source, this may lead to anxiety and susceptibility to the confirmation bias. Finally, searching sources such as books and the Internet may directly increase health anxiety simply by exposing the person to exaggerations and misinformation about dreaded diseases. However, because checking and reassurance-seeking sometimes produce a temporary reduction in anxiety or uncertainty, this behavior is negatively reinforced and becomes a habit.

Checking and seeking reassurances are key symptoms in health anxiety that make the problem persist

Body checking, which doctors sometimes encourage in case of a possible health problem (e.g., "let me know if it feels worse"), maintains health anxiety by promoting hypervigilance and possibly the discovery of new "symptoms." Some types of body checking can actually *induce* the "symptoms" of the feared illness. For example, continually manipulating an ordinary skin mole can lead to infection and the appearance of something more serious (e.g., melanoma). Also, frequently palpating a lymph node to check for tenderness can in fact *cause* tenderness. Because the health anxious person is most likely to check his or her body when feeling anxious (i.e., during anxious arousal), he or she is especially likely to notice body sensations. For example, one medically healthy woman we evaluated only used her blood pressure cuff to measure this vital sign *when she was feeling anxious about her blood pressure.* Ironically, her anxiety temporarily raised her blood pressure every time she took the measurement! Thus, she believed (falsely) that she suffered from cardiovascular disease.

Avoidance. Avoidance of illness-related cues (e.g., mosquitoes) temporarily reduces or terminates exposure to anxiety and perceived threats (e.g., West Nile virus), thus reducing fear in the short-term. In the long-term, however, habitual avoidance maintains health anxiety by preventing experiences that can correct mistaken beliefs and interpretations of health-related stimuli (e.g., most mosquitoes do not carry the West Nile virus). Since avoidance, like safety behaviors and signals, reduces anxiety in the short-run, it is reinforced and becomes stronger and more widespread with time. Thus, health anxious individuals come to perceive these behaviors as necessary for coping with anxiety and avoiding serious illnesses.

2.3   Treatment Implications of the Model

The biopsychosocial model of health anxiety forms the basis for effective treatment

The biopsychosocial model leads to specific targets for reducing health anxiety. In particular, effective treatment must help patients (a) correct maladaptive health- and illness-related beliefs and interpretations of benign bodily sensations that lead to exaggerated health concerns and (b) decrease behaviors that prevent the self-correction of these maladaptive beliefs and interpretations. The task of cognitive-behavior therapy (CBT) is therefore to foster an evaluation of bodily sensations and variations as non-threatening, and not demanding further attention, reassurance, or action. Patients must come to understand their problem not in terms of the risk of having an undiagnosed medical condition, or how they can prevent such catastrophes, but rather in terms of how they are misperceiving generally harmless bodily stimuli and responding excessively in ways that perpetuate their misperceptions. In Chapter 4 we outline a treatment program designed to address these implications

3

Diagnosis and Treatment Indications

This chapter provides a framework for conducting a thorough diagnostic assessment and introducing the patient to the psychological approach to treating health anxiety. The biopsychosocial model and its treatment implications (see Chapter 2) guide the assessment, and the initial consultation provides an excellent opportunity to build rapport with health anxious individuals who may be accustomed to a *medical* approach and may be opposed to a *psychological* approach.

3.1   Review of Medical Records

Many health anxious patients have a history of visiting physicians, and therefore usually have an extensive record of medical consultations, exams, and procedures. We recommend reviewing this information as soon as possible, preferably before the initial visit, in order to be aware of any actual medical conditions that the patient may have. Additionally, a thorough medical record review may reveal information that has already been communicated to the patient by his or her physician or by other healthcare professionals.

It is important to be familiar with the patient's medical history

3.2   Self-Report Inventories

To assess self-reported psychological distress we recommend that the patient complete the SHAI and CBHQ (described in Chapter 1) as part of the initial evaluation. Other self-report measures, such as the Beck Depression Inventory-II (BDI-II; Beck, Steer, & Brown, 1996), Patient Health Questionnaire (PHQ-9; Spitzer, Kroenke, & Williams, 1999) or Depression, Anxiety and Stress Scale (DASS; Lovibond & Lovibond, 1995) can also be administered. It should be noted that patients who strongly believe their complaints (e.g., anxiety) have a medical basis, and who are resistant to a psychological approach, may minimize their psychological complaints (e.g., anxiety) on these self-report forms. Thus, these questionnaires are best used in conjunction with interview and behavioral data.

How to conduct a
clinical interview for
severe health anxiety

3.3   The Clinical Interview

> **Clinical Pearl**
> **Reducing the Patient's Defensiveness**
>
> Terms such as "hypochondriasis," "anxiety," and "somatization" have negative connotations for many patients. To reduce defensiveness, refer to the patient's problem as "unexplained physical (or medical) symptoms."

3.3.1   Chief Complaint and History

We begin the assessment by asking the patient to describe his or her reasons for, and thoughts and feelings about, attending the session. Although many patients believe their symptoms have at least some psychological basis and are open to seeing a mental health professional, some attend merely to appease medical doctors or family members and may view the appointment as their chance to convince others that the problem is not "all in their head." Regardless of the reason for attending, the patient will welcome the opportunity to discuss his or her feelings about seeing a mental health professional.

Most patients will probably have already been told, perhaps many times from different medical personnel, that their physical health is fine. Most people are delighted by such news, but health anxious patients tend to feel belittled by these reports or believe that they are being ignored (e.g., "No one will listen to me! I'm really sick!"). The mental health practitioner's task is to (a) validate that such experiences may lead to feelings of frustration, (b) acknowledge the physical signs and sensations as *real* as opposed to "in their head," and (c) align the patient towards wanting to improve their overall well-being *in addition to* finding relief from their physical concerns. Relevant data about the onset and course of the problem, and about the patient's social, developmental personal, and family history should also be obtained.

> **Clinical Pearl**
> **Example of a Typical Day**
>
> It is often helpful to ask the patient to describe a typical day, highlighting the frequency, intensity, and duration of body symptoms, health concerns, and behaviors performed in response to these concerns (e.g., "What do you do when you notice the pain in your abdomen?"). The interviewer should assess what cues the episodes, how the patient tries to manage the problem, how the symptoms interfere with functioning, and any behaviors that might reinforce the health-related anxiety.

3.3.2   Mood

Since health anxious individuals often suffer from frustration, irritability, and depressive symptoms, mood state should be assessed. Patients may deny mood symptoms; therefore, it is often helpful to normalize these feelings and phrase questions with the assumption that they are present (e.g., "With all that you've been through with your doctors, you must be pretty upset. Tell me what that's been like for you"). Having the patient rate his or her mood on a scale from 0 (bad mood) to 10 (very good mood) can also be useful.

3.3.3 Social Functioning

Many health anxious patients have difficulties with occupational and social functioning and with close personal relationships. The degree of impairment in these and other areas of daily living should be assessed.

3.3.4 History and Previous Treatment

Circumstances surrounding the onset and course of the problem should be assessed (e.g., "When did you first notice the disconcerting body symptoms? When did you start seeking reassurance and checking with doctors?"). Fortunately, it is not essential to know the exact causes or predisposing factors of health anxiety in order for treatment to be successful. Nevertheless, if the patient has a hypothesis about this, it can be both validating and informative to discuss this information. For example, symptoms might have started following a personal experience with illness, or a family member's diagnosis.

It is also helpful to inquire about previous treatment, especially mental health treatment. Perhaps medications or supportive or psychodynamic therapy has been tried. If former treatment providers have given the patient incorrect information (e.g., that hypochondriasis is caused by unresolved childhood conflicts), this can be addressed by providing corrective information.

3.3.5 Family Issues

What was that patient's family of origin and upbringing like? Did any relatives suffer with medical problems or psychological disorders? How did the parents react when someone became ill? Could catastrophic messages about health and illness have been learned from the family of origin? Such experiences can set the stage for the development of health anxiety by fostering maladaptive core beliefs. For example, many patients with concerns about cancer have family members who died of cancer.

Assessment should also address relatives' responses to the patient's health anxiety. In some families, relatives are critical and hostile toward loved ones with unsubstantiated health complaints. In others, relatives enable or accommodate the health anxiety symptoms by providing frequent reassurance and by helping the patient avoid situations that evoke distress. When possible, include family members in the assessment. This allows the clinician to observe how the patient and significant other interact and also provides another point of view on the problem. For example, a close relative can often provide a more objective report on how the family is affected by the patient's difficulties.

3.4   Identifying the Appropriate Treatment

Effective treatments
for health anxiety
have been identified
in research studies

Two types of treatments have been studied for health anxiety: cognitive behavior therapy (CBT) and certain types of pharmacotherapy, primarily selective serotonin reuptake inhibitors (SSRIs). This section briefly describes these treatments and their advantages and disadvantages.

3.4.1   Medications

Several case studies and a small number of controlled trials suggest that antidepressant medications, including SSRIs, can be effective in reducing health anxiety and related symptoms (Fallon, 2001). However, placebo responsivity tends to be high in health anxiety (Fallon et al., 1996), thus the precise mechanism of action for these drugs is not well understood. Table 7 lists the medications that have been studied, along with their recommended doses.

Advantages and
disadvantages of
medication for
health anxiety

Advantages of Medication
- Generally safe and easy to use
- Potentially clinically effective
- Easily accessible (they can be prescribed by any physician – although psychiatrists are preferable)
- Requires minimal follow-up (compared to weekly therapy sessions)

Disadvantages of Medication
- Limited improvement on average
- Possible side effects
- Health anxious patients are often extremely sensitive to drug side effects
- Must be used continuously to sustain any improvement

Table 7
Medications with Initial Empirical Support for Health Anxiety

Medication	Recommended dose	Studies
Clomipramine	25–225 mg/d	Kamlana & Gray (1988); Stone (1993)
Imipramine	125–150 mg/d	Lippert (1986); Wesner & Noyes, (1991) [not in reference list]
Fluoxetine	20–80 mg/d	Fallon, (1999); Fallon, Javitch, Hollander, & Liebowitz (1991); Fallon et al. (1993, 1996)
Fluvoxamine	300 mg/d	Fallon (2001); Fallon et al. (1996, 2003)
Paroxetine	Up to 60 mg/d	Greeven et al. (2007); Oosterbaan, van Balkom, van Boeijen, de Meij, & van Dyck (2001)
Nefazodone	200–500 mg/d	Kjernisted, Enns, & Lander (2002)

3.4.2 Cognitive Behavior Therapy (CBT)

CBT is a skills-based intervention that teaches patients healthy ways of thinking and behaving to reverse the vicious cycles involved in health anxiety that are described in Chapter 2. Specifically, CBT aims to help patients recognize and modify faulty health-related beliefs and perceptions, and eliminate avoidance, checking, and reassurance-seeking behaviors that prevent the correction of faulty beliefs. The essential components of CBT (which are illustrated in Chapter 4) include (a) psychoeducation, (b) cognitive therapy techniques, (c) exposure therapy, and (d) response prevention.

The **psychoeducational component** entails socializing the patient to the biopsychosocial model (from Chapter 2) and providing a rationale for how treatment addresses health-related concerns from this perspective. **Cognitive techniques** involve rational discussion to help the patient identify and correct mistaken beliefs about health and illness, avoidance, and safety-seeking (checking, reassurance-seeking) behaviors.

Components of cognitive-behavioral therapy for health anxiety

Exposure therapy includes a set of techniques that help patients gradually confront those stimuli that evoke anxiety. **Situational (or *in vivo*) exposure** entails gradually confronting external fear triggers, such as hospitals and newspaper, web, or magazine articles about feared illnesses. **Interoceptive exposure** entails purposely confronting feared bodily sensations, such as stomach aches and feeling tired. The patient remains exposed to the feared stimulus until associated anxiety decreases on its own, without attempting to reduce the distress by withdrawing from the situation, seeking reassurance, or using other safety behaviors. Thus, the **response prevention** component of CBT entails refraining from any behaviors that serve as an escape from health-related anxiety or uncertainty.

As with medication treatment, there are advantages and disadvantages to CBT. These are as follows.

Advantages of CBT
- Clinically effective: 50%–60% symptom reduction on average
- Treatment is fairly brief (usually 16–20 sessions)
- Long-term maintenance of treatment gains

Disadvantages of CBT
- Patient must work hard to achieve improvement
- Involves purposely evoking anxiety during exposure
- Not widely available

Advantages and disadvantages of CBT for health anxiety

3.5 Factors that Influence Treatment Decisions

Very little research is available to inform decisions regarding which type of treatment to recommend for a particular patient with health anxiety. Medication and CBT can be used simultaneously. Our clinical experience with many patients who become concerned about medication side effects suggests that CBT should be the first line treatment for all age groups with health anxiety. Compared to young and middle-aged adults, children and the elderly tend to have more difficulty with adherence to medication. The elderly are more

What form of treatment is best for whom?

vulnerable to drug side effects due to reduced metabolic rate and possible interactions with other medications. Family conflict can also interfere with CBT, especially in young adults with close family ties. Males and females respond equally well to CBT.

Successful CBT requires that the patient grasp the theoretical model of health anxiety and rationale for treatment. Patients must also be able to complete treatment exercises on their own. These tasks may be difficult for individuals who are very concrete in their thinking. Medication is recommended for developmentally disabled and cognitively impaired patients, although a modified CBT program can be effective in these populations. Patients with poor insight into the senselessness of their health concerns may be reluctant to engage in CBT and have difficulty consolidating the information learned from using these techniques. As a result, medication might be necessary for such individuals.

Patient preference for a particular treatment modality should be strongly considered. Reviewing the advantages and disadvantages of each approach allows patients to make an informed decision about which therapy they would prefer to receive. Greater adherence to either treatment, especially CBT, can be expected from patients who agree willingly to a particular plan, as opposed to those situations in which they are coerced by others (or forced) into treatment.

Although it may be beneficial for patients to identify a relative or close friend to provide support during CBT, this is not always essential. Such a confidant should be firm, relaxed, and empathic. Emotionally over-involved, hostile, and inconsistent confidants can lead to attrition. Before enlisting a specific support person to help with CBT, one should assess how this person interacts with the patient.

3.6   Presenting the Recommendation for CBT

Recommending a psychological treatment approach may be challenging if the patient rejects the need for anything other than medical attention

This section describes how to present CBT to a patient. Because some patients initially reject psychological explanations and treatments for their perceived medical problems, the strategies we present are designed to help build acceptance of this framework without appearing as if trying to convince the patient that a psychological approach is necessary. In general, these techniques are consistent with motivational interviewing which has been shown to be effective in helping patients prepare for behavior change.

3.6.1   Getting a Foot in the Door

Establish that the patient's physical complaints, themselves, are authentic

Convey acceptance of the physical complaints as authentic and begin the conversation by asking nonjudgmental questions that allow the patient to express his or her feelings about the role of medical versus psychological factors. For example, "In light of what your doctors are saying, what percent out of 100% of your health issues do you think are due to medical factors; versus what percent might be due to some sort of psychological factors?" Most patients will concede that psychological factors account for *some* of their symptoms (even if only 10%), which opens the door for a discussion about the role of such factors (e.g., "So, you say '80% medical and 20% psychological'. How do you think *psychological* factors might play a role in your health problems, even if they are only 20%?"). Gain the patient's permission to discuss psychological factors further. For example, "Since I'm not a physician, would it be OK if today we focus on the 20% of your symptoms that might be related to psychological factors?"

3.6.2   The Mind-Body Connection

Help the patient consider how his or her thinking and behavior can affect physical symptoms. For patients who minimize the role of psychological factors, cloak references to psychological processes, such as anxiety, within the concept of the "mind-body connection." For example, explain the "fight-or-flight" response as a normal reaction to feeling that something isn't quite right about one's health that can produce uncomfortable "side effects" such as feeling tired, dizzy, out of breath, nauseous, and sometimes even ringing in the ears, blurred vision, and the sensation of choking. Thus, at the very moment one perceives a symptom and becomes concerned about it, *more* body symptoms occur due to the mind-body connection.

Thinking and behavior influence bodily sensations

3.6.3   Body Vigilance and Body Noise

Point out that it is normal for someone concerned about his or her health to pay close attention, and even monitor, his or her body. Also, point out that even healthy bodies produce noticeable sensations and perturbations or body noise. Although body noise is noticeable and sometimes intense or uncomfortable, it is not necessarily an indication of a serious medical illness. Yet, if someone is constantly monitoring his or her body, he or she will be sensitive to even normal body noise, which could lead to the fear that there is a medical problem.

People with health anxiety pay close attention to their bodies and therefore are exquisitely sensitive to even benign changes in bodily states

3.6.4   Effects of Behavioral Responses

Using the information presented in Chapter 2, help the patient to gain a new perspective on behaviors such as frequently discussing health issues, looking up information on the Internet, avoidance, body checking, and doctor shopping. Rather than *solutions*, these behaviors are actually part of the *problem*. A helpful strategy is to discuss both the advantages and disadvantages of these behaviors, and the pros and cons of stopping them. Point out that although responding in this way to bodily concerns may reduce discomfort and uncertainty in the short term, it leads to a greater focus on the body, and can even exacerbate body noise in the long run.

3.6.5   Presenting the Treatment Rationale

It is important to present a credible and coherent rationale for treatment

The following points should be clearly conveyed to the patient (and family members if appropriate) when discussing the possibility of CBT:

- Review the data collected during the interview that suggest the presence of health anxiety.
- Define health anxiety and review the signs and symptoms as discussed in Chapter 1. Use the patient's own symptoms as examples. Emphasize that health anxiety is a chronic problem that is unlikely to get better without effective treatment.
- Explain that the exact causes of health anxiety are unknown. Emphasize that numerous factors (biological and environmental/learning) probably contribute together to the cause of this problem.
- Convey that effective treatment does not require that we know the causes, but only that we understand the signs and symptoms of health anxiety. Fortunately, after much research, we have come to understand these symptoms very well.
- Describe CBT as a form of treatment that aims to reduce the symptoms of health anxiety, regardless of their cause. Specifically, CBT aims to ameliorate two maladaptive patterns: (a) becoming excessively anxious over certain bodily symptoms and the possibility of illness, and (b) using checking, reassurance-seeking, avoidance and other maladaptive behaviors to cope with the health concerns. Give examples of the patient's signs and symptoms to illustrate these patterns.
- Using the information in section 3.4 as a guide, describe psychoeducation, cognitive therapy, exposure techniques and relapse prevention techniques. Inform the patient that treatment involves learning skills, and provide a few examples of the kinds of techniques that might be used in treatment.
- Explain that during exposure therapy, the patient can expect to become anxious, but that the anxiety is temporary and it subsides with practice. During treatment, the therapist will help the patient learn healthier ways of thinking and responding to anxiety-evoking situations.
- Assure the patient that you realize CBT is hard work. Review the advantages and disadvantages of this approach.
- Stress that the therapy process is a collaborative one. Use the analogy of the therapist as a coach. You will help the patient to learn and use skills to reduce health anxiety. You will never force or surprise the patient with exposure tasks.
- Ensure that the patient understands the amount of benefit a person gets from CBT is related to how much effort they put into treatment.
- Recommend a trial of 16 sessions of CBT and answer any questions from the patient and family members.

3.6.6   Eliciting "Change Talk"

How to help the patient make his or her own arguments for engaging in therapy

Whether the patient responds in a positive or negative manner to the biopsychosocial model and treatment rationale, starting this sort of a treatment is a delicate process that usually involves some degree of ambivalence. The decision to engage in treatment might occur gradually, and the clinician must not confuse the decision-making *process* with an actual *decision*. Throughout this process the therapist should try to elicit *from the patient* arguments in favor

Table 8
Topics and Questions for Eliciting Change Talk from Patients with Health Anxiety

Topic	Sample questions
Disadvantages of the status quo	• How have your unexplained symptoms interfered with your life? • What bothers you the most when your physicians cannot find a medical explanation for your symptoms?
Advantages of change	• How would life be different if you didn't need an explanation for every symptom your body produces? • What are some of the advantages of being medically healthy?
Optimism about change	• What difficult challenges have you overcome in the past?
Intent to change	• How important is it for you to get some help for your unexplained medical symptoms?
Negative extremes	• What would the rest of your life be like if your doctors never gave you an adequate explanation for these symptoms? • How much more time and money are you willing to spend on doctor appointments if they only make you more frustrated?
Positive extremes	• How would life be different if you could control these symptoms better? • How will the other people in your life react when you can manage these symptoms in more helpful ways?

of a psychological approach; but without advocating too strongly for change. The latter can paradoxically result in the patient coming up with his or her own arguments for not changing his/her thoughts and behaviors. "Change talk" (Amrhein, Miller, Yahne, Palmer, & Fulcher, 2003) includes statements by the patient that reflect commitment, desire, perceived ability, need, readiness, or reasons to change. Miller and Rollnick (2002) suggest eliciting change talk by asking questions that force the patient to consider the topics in Table 8.

Another strategy is to discuss with the patient the perceived short and long-term pros and cons of psychological treatment. Engaging in such treatment might have a number of short-term disadvantages (e.g., trying a non-medical approach), whereas the advantages are more long-term and can be difficult to envision (e.g., not requiring a medical explanation). On the other hand, avoiding treatment might have short-term advantages for the patient (e.g., keeping a medical focus), but is disadvantageous in the long-term (e.g., functional impairment). Advantages of therapy can be increased in scope, and disadvantages can be gently challenged. The patient has a choice to remain at the status quo or to try a new approach that is very much at odds with his or her view of the problem.

A third approach is to discuss the length of time the patient has devoted to pursuing a medical explanation for his or her complaints and how effective this pursuit has been in solving the problem. The therapist can then point out that the patient has little to lose by engaging in an alternative or augmentative psychological treatment approach. If the psychological approach does not turn out to be helpful, he or she can return to the previous strategy.

4

Treatment

4.1   Methods of Treatment

This chapter presents the details of how to plan and implement a CBT program for health anxiety. Table 9 shows the optimal schedule for what is to be accomplished in each treatment session. In the interest of flexibility, however, the focus of this chapter is on mastery of the particular treatment strategies rather than on promoting a strict session-by-session agenda.

The "nuts and bolts" of conducting CBT for health anxiety

Table 9
Suggested Structure of Psychological Treatment for Health Anxiety

Session 1
- Begin functional assessment of health anxiety symptoms
- Introduce self-monitoring
- Begin psychoeducation

Session 2
- Continue functional assessment
- Review psychoeducational material
- Introduce cognitive therapy

Session 3
- Review psychoeducational material
- Cognitive therapy

Session 4
- Cognitive therapy
- Begin planning for exposure and response prevention

Sessions 5–10
- Exposure
- Response prevention
- Cognitive therapy

Sessions 11–14
- Exposure (emphasis on patient as his/her own therapist)
- Response prevention
- Cognitive therapy

Sessions 15 & 16
- End response prevention
- Discussion of proper health behaviors and self-care
- Arrange for follow-up care (as necessary)

4.1.1   Functional Assessment

**Functional
assessment – the
collecting of
detailed, patient-
specific information**

A functional assessment is the collection of detailed, patient-specific information about health anxiety triggers and the cognitive and behavioral responses to these triggers. The biopsychosocial conceptualization described in Chapter 2 dictates what information is collected and how it is organized to form a treatment plan. The Functional Assessment Form (Appendix 1) can be used to document this information in an organized fashion. Typically, this assessment lasts from 1 to 2 hours. Begin by explaining that a complete understanding of health anxiety symptoms is necessary to tailor the treatment program to the patient's specific needs.

Assessing Triggers

**What internal and
external stimuli cue
episodes of health
anxiety?**

Generate a complete list of external and internal stimuli that evoke health-related anxiety, uncertainty, or distress. These stimuli might be used as the basis of exposure exercises.

Bodily Signs, Sensations, and Perturbations. Obtain a list of the bodily signs, sensations, perturbations, and variations that trigger episodes of health anxiety. Signs and sensations might be internal, but can also be associated with the skin, hair, or products that are expelled from the body. Questions to elicit this information include:
- Which bodily symptoms are you concerned with?
- What kinds of symptoms provoke concerns about your health?

In addition, the patient can be asked to record the incidence of each feared sensation for one week, including symptom severity and the situation in which it occurred. A monitoring form for this use appears in Appendix 2. For some individuals, the feared sensations will be circumscribed around a particular region of the body (e.g., abdomen), organ system (e.g., digestive), or bodily function (e.g., swallowing). For others, feared sensations might be diverse. Regardless, this structured self-monitoring will provide the therapist and patient with invaluable assessment information.

External Situations and Stimuli. Information about the full range of external situations and stimuli that trigger preoccupation with health and illness should also be identified. Such triggers often include hospitals, doctors, seeing or hearing about sick people, reading about illnesses, and other stimuli that serve as reminders of health concerns. Being alone or "too far" from a hospital or medical center can also be situational triggers, as can seeing oneself naked or giving oneself an examination (e.g., breast or testicular). Most patients are well aware of, and most forthcoming in describing, the stimuli that trigger heath preoccupation. Key assessment questions include:
- What situations trigger your health-related thoughts and concerns?
- What situations do you avoid because they might trigger your health concerns?

Assessing Cognitive Features

Obtaining information about the following cognitive aspects of the patient's health concerns will help in developing an effective treatment plan.

Misinterpretations of Bodily Signs and Sensations. Inquire about the patient's beliefs concerning the presence and meaning of unexpected, unwanted, or disconcerting bodily sensations. For example, "when my head hurts, I think I'm getting a brain tumor" or "When I feel a lump in my throat, it reminds me that I have a serious neck problem that no doctors have been able to figure out." Examples of questions to elicit this information include:

- What do you think this symptom means?
- What do you feel is causing you to have this symptom?

Feared Cconsequences. Assess the patient's beliefs about the probability and severity of becoming ill, being in pain, or even dying. Some patients have specific fears of explicit disastrous consequences; whereas for others, the internal and external cues evoke only a vague sense that "something is wrong." Specifically inquiring about the following could be helpful:

- Given your symptoms, what is the *worst* thing that will happen? How will this occur? Who will be involved? What could be done (if anything) to stop it?

Dysfunctional Health-Related Beliefs. Assess the various domains dysfunctional health-related beliefs described in Table 5 in Chapter 2. Not all of these types of beliefs may be present, yet an understanding of those that are will help the therapist focus on the cognitive therapy element of treatment.

Assessing Behavioral Responses to Health Anxiety

It is important to identify maladaptive behaviors the patient uses in response to health anxiety to cope with or reduce uncertainty, anxiety, and the threat of illness. These behaviors will be targeted in the exposure and response prevention components of CBT.

Avoidance. Avoidance patterns are patient-specific, but often include staying away from hospitals, people with certain illnesses or diseases, funerals, and cemeteries. Patients might avoid health or disease-related movies, TV shows, news articles, and other information in the media. Discussions of disease, death, and dying might also be avoided, as might physical exertion or other activities believed to "overly stress the body." Whereas some health anxious patients engage in excessive body checking and doctor shopping (see the upcoming sections on checking and reassurance-seeking), others *avoid* these activities for fear that the presence of an illness will be confirmed. A patient's avoidance behavior can often be predicted from his or her triggers and feared consequences. For example, the fear of rabies might lead to avoidance of certain animals; preoccupation with cancer might lead to avoidance of media stories covering this topic. Questions to assess avoidance include:

- What kinds of things do you not do because of your concerns about _____?
- What situations do you routinely avoid?

It is also important to assess the cognitive basis of avoidance, that is, *why* the experience is avoided. A good way to access this information is to inquire about what might happen if the situation or trigger could not be avoided (e.g., "what do you fear would happen if you could not avoid _____?").

> **Identify ways in which the patient misinterprets the presence and meaning of unexplained bodily sensations or perturbations**

> **What would happen if...?**

> **Determine the patient's maladaptive responses to bodily sensations and health-related concerns**

Body monitoring and checking may be overt or covert and are important to carefully assess

Body Monitoring and Checking. Assess the frequency, duration, and method of body checking and monitoring. Such checking can be extensive and might include examination of the body's vital signs (sometimes using medical equipment that the patient has purchased for just this purpose) or examining the structure and function of a particular body part. For example, prodding at blemishes on their skin, probing bodily orifices digitally or with tools (e.g., a dentist's mirror), and closely inspecting (e.g., smelling) certain body parts or bodily excretions for "normalcy." Obtain a full description of each checking behavior (some of which might be embarrassing for the patient to describe) and inquire as to whether others are involved in the checking (e.g., does a family member help to inspect or monitor?). Given the potential for embarrassment, it is important to create a safe and supportive environment for the patient so that he or she feels comfortable fully sharing these behaviors.

As with avoidance, it is important to know the relationship between body checking and health anxiety. Inquiry might include questions such as:

- What purpose does the body checking serve?
- What might happen if you don't check?
- How do you check your body for symptoms of this illness? What exactly do you do?
- How often do you check in this way?
- How do you feel after you have checked yourself?
- How does this sort of checking keep you safe?

Answers to these questions will help the therapist understand the basis for the behavior, which is typically a distorted belief or assumption that can be challenged later in therapy (e.g., "If I don't check my testicles every day I won't notice that I have testicular cancer until it is too late").

Checking and reassurance-seeking may take many different forms

Reassurance-Seeking via Other Forms of Checking. Assess for other forms of checking and reassurance-seeking, such as extraneous doctor visits for the same complaints, repeatedly asking health professionals and relatives for opinions about the same health issues, repetitively reviewing medical test results and reports, and searching medical texts and Internet sites for information about the diseases of concern. Collect information about the intensity, frequency, and duration of these behaviors, and the extent to which others are involved. The following questions can help in the assessment of reassurance-seeking:

- How often do you read about the symptoms or the feared illness?
- Where do you get your information about the symptoms or illness?
- Do you ever look your symptoms up in medical textbooks, on the internet, or other sources?
- How is your relationship with doctors? Do you repeatedly ask them the same questions? Do you ask for tests to be repeated? Has a doctor ever fired you?
- How is your relationship with your friends and family? How often do you ask them about your symptoms?
- What medical tests or procedures have you undergone in order to rule out the illness or get a better explanation for the symptoms? Have you had these tests more than once?
- What kinds of checking behaviors do you have that relate to your symptoms?

- Are there other things you do to seek reassurance that you do/do not have this illness?

Miscellaneous Safety Behaviors and Signals. Safety *behaviors* are actions the person engages in to reduce anxiety or fear. Examples include the use of a cane in a man with the fear that his leg bones were "rotting," and being sure to get eight hours of sleep because of the fear that lack of sleep would precipitate a specific serious illness. Safety *signals* are situations or objects that the patient associates with safety, perhaps because of the fear of imminent incapacitation or death. Examples include cell phones, medications, a Medic Alert bracelet, and medical facilities. Many patients do not recognize these behaviors, situations, or objects as part of their problem, especially if they have become routine or could be justified in other ways (e.g., carrying a cell phone is necessary to stay in touch with people). Questions to help elucidate safety behaviors and signals are:

- Are there things you do to protect yourself from _____ (specify disease or condition)? What are they?
- Are there things you do to make yourself feel more comfortable or to reduce symptoms? Like what?
- Do you carry anything with you to help you feel safe about your health?
- What precautions do you take so that you are prepared if you should have a medical emergency (such as a cell phone, safe person, certain medications, remaining close to hospitals/medical centers)?

Clinical Pearl
The Play-by-Play Description

To gain additional insight into the patient's experience of health anxiety, and how he or she copes with symptoms, ask for a "play-by-play" description of a few specific instances. This technique could also be used to focus the assessment on a particular symptom that might be difficult to understand. It involves asking questions such as, "What were you doing when you noticed the symptoms occurring?" The patient is then asked to step through the situation and report their emotional and cognitive responses: What were you feeling and thinking? How strong was your fear or worry? What did you do next? How did you cope with the symptoms? Did you check or seek reassurance? How did the situation resolve itself and how did you feel afterwards? It is helpful to point out the relationships among symptoms, uncertainty, and increased anxiety; and between reassurance-seeking and anxiety reduction. Illustrating this relationship to the patient can instill hope in the therapy program, as well as a sense of trust in your expertise.

Ask the patient for a "play-by-play" description of health anxiety episodes to illustrate a typical example

---

Clinical Pearl
The Patient-Therapist Relationship

In CBT, the relationship between patient and therapist is analogous to that between a student and a teacher, or between an athlete and a coach. It is helpful to explain this at the beginning of therapy to set expectations for the course of treatment. Below is a sample explanation of this relationship:

The therapeutic relationship is an important part of CBT because it lays the foundation for the patient to be able to successfully learn the skills necessary to overcome health anxiety

Clinical Pearl
continued

It is best to think of me as your coach. Let's say you wanted to learn to play a musical instrument like the drums. You would go to a drum teacher who would give you instructions and then watch you play to look for things that you need to work on. The teacher would then help you improve your technique and tell you to practice hard between lessons. Now, if you didn't practice the new techniques, or if you practiced them in a different way from the way the teacher taught you, you would not develop the skills needed to be a good drummer. Also, the teacher would not force you to practice – you would decide whether or not to practice. If you didn't practice, the teacher might encourage you to practice more, but eventually he or she might stop the lessons if it was clear that you weren't practicing enough.

Our relationship works the same way. I know how to teach you different skills that are designed especially for you to reduce your problems with health concerns. If you practice the exercises I show you and learn the skills, chances are you will see improvement. But, if you decide not to practice them as much as you should, or if you decide to change the exercises around, chances are you will not improve as much as you would like. I have a great deal of confidence in this treatment. But, I cannot force you to do the exercises and learn the skills – this is your therapy and the decision has to come from you. We are on the same team against health anxiety. If you do the hard work in therapy, you will find that my coaching and support is very helpful.

4.1.2   Self Monitoring

Self-monitoring is an important (yet often overlooked) component of CBT

To aid the functional assessment, ask the patient to use the Symptom Record Form (Appendix 3) to keep a real-time log of triggers that lead to health concerns and reassurance-seeking behaviors. Explain the form's importance and give instructions for completing it. Some patients fail to carefully and accurately self-monitor because they do not appreciate the task's relevance to treatment. Many see the task as "busy work" or irrelevant. To increase adherence, convey the following:

- Keeping track using the form helps both the therapist and the patient gain an accurate picture of the extent of the problem, as well as the situations and symptoms that lead to health concerns.
- These data help the patient identify triggers and maladaptive behaviors that he or she might not be aware of.
- Some patients use the fact that they have to report their reassurance-seeking behaviors to the therapist as motivation to resist the behaviors associated with health anxiety.
- Accurate reporting of these episodes between now and the end of treatment will reveal how much progress is made.
- To avoid forgetting important details, each episode should be recorded *immediately*, rather than waiting until the end of the day.

It may help to review an actual recent episode or (an imaginary one), having the patient practice recording this information on the form. To further increase adherence, tell the patient that the first item on the agenda for the next session will be to review the Symptom Record Forms.

4.1.3   Psychoeducation

The educational component of CBT provides the patient a foundation for understanding his or her problem as involving maladaptive thinking and behavioral patterns, rather than as a medical condition that must be fully explained and treated. Additionally, it teaches the patient how he or she can get relief by using CBT. There are four psychoeducation modules, which cover: (a) body noise and body vigilance, (b) the fight-flight response, (c) the effects of thinking "threatening thoughts", and (d) the effects of safety behaviors. Although the psychoeducational sessions occur early in therapy, it is common to review this material with the patient throughout the course of treatment.

Psychoeducation helps socialize the patient to the biopsychosocial approach to health anxiety

---

Clinical Pearl
Considering the Patient's Perspective

Since many patients with health anxiety believe their physicians have written them off without fully listening to their complaints, we begin by asking patients whether any questions remain from the previous visit, and whether there might be anything further to add to the functional assessment. Next, if not yet expressed, we ask the patient for his or her understanding of the unexplained symptoms, their causes, and how he or she feels about doctors' impressions and the results of lab tests that have been conducted. To show consideration for the patient's perspective, the therapist suggests treating this viewpoint as one possible explanation for the problem that should neither be ruled out nor accepted unconditionally without exploring other hypotheses. This sets the stage for presenting educational information based on the biopsychosocial model.

Body Noise and Body Vigilance

Health anxious patients are often looking for answers to the question, "If I am not medically ill, why do I even have symptoms?" Thus, it is helpful to begin psychoeducation by teaching the patient about the many possible benign sources of bodily sensations and perturbations ("symptoms"), and about the effects of paying excessive attention to one's body. The Our Noisy Bodies handout (Appendix 4) contains such information and can be given to the patient to read and discuss during the session. Alternatively, the therapist can summarize this information in session and assign the handout for further reading. Either way, the therapist should be able to speak with authority about the information in this handout.

When we become anxious about something, we naturally tend to pay more attention to it

At the same time, the clinician must be careful to not appear as if he or she is trying to definitively explain all of the patient's medically unexplained symptoms. Doing so could be viewed as discounting the patient's concerns, and could lead to resistance. Psychoeducation merely aims to open the patient's mind to *possible* alternative explanations about the origin of symptoms. Later in therapy, the patient will conduct tests and collect evidence for these various hypotheses.

Sources of Body Symptoms. Present the following key concepts to help the patient consider alternative explanations for the causes of their bodily sensations and perturbations.

- Bodily perturbations, sensations, and variations not accounted for by medical problems might originate from normal homeostatic processes as the body works to keep a stable and optimal internal environment. Ironically, this is a sign of a healthy body!
- Sensations can also arise due to changes in routine, such as changes in sleep-wake schedule, engaging in atypical levels of activity, changes in diet and timing of meals, and changes in emotional well-being (the effects of anxious arousal are covered in the section on the fight-or-flight response).
- *Minor* medical conditions such as colds, asthma, and allergies can produce benign bodily symptoms ranging from hives, to a dry or sore throat, to lightheadedness, pounding heart, headaches, and nausea.
- These causes of body sensations will not show up on most medical exams or lab tests because they are considered "normal" despite the fact that they can produce noticeable "symptoms." Medical tests are typically designed to yield a positive result only when a condition is in need of medical treatment. Thus, a negative test result (suggesting good health) is not the same as saying that no symptoms are present. It simply indicates that the symptoms are not caused by a serious clinical condition. This explains the existence of symptoms despite medical feedback suggesting no serious illness.

Body Vigilance. Discuss how focusing attention on body symptoms leads to increased detection of bodily noise, resulting in a greater chance of feeling medically ill. The following key points are important to mention:

- The more someone pays attention to a particular bodily sensation, the more noteworthy it will seem and the more unpleasant and ominous it will appear.
- As the person spends more time scrutinizing his or her body, he or she begins to notice and attend to subtle details of body sensations, and becomes adept at making finer and finer discriminations. As people notice subtle differences in their body sensations, they may perceive that "new" symptoms are emerging and that their health seems to be deteriorating. This, of course, leads to increased anxiety, additional sensations (associated with emotional arousal), greater body vigilance, and a self-perpetuating vicious cycle.
- Point out the inter-relationship of body noise and body vigilance: noticing strange body sensations (i.e., body noise) triggers health concerns, which evokes more body vigilance, which leads to increased perception of body noise. The cycle gets stronger with each repetition. Patients can be asked how they have experienced this cycle.

The Fight-Or-Flight Response

The fight-or-flight response is a normal and adaptive response to the perception of threat

In this educational module, the aim is to normalize the experience of anxiety (worry, fear, stress) and help the patient understand how it plays a part in his or her problem.

What Is Anxiety? The dialogue below illustrates how to begin discussing the patient's definition of "anxiety" and convey that anxiety is actually an adaptive and protective mechanism:

T: How would you define "anxiety"?

P: I don't know... going crazy, out of control, mental disorder.

T: Do you think anxiety can be good?

P: No, it's bad. It's like being crazy.

T: OK. So, what would happen if you had an important job interview and you experienced absolutely no anxiety at all?

P: Hmm. I think I see what you mean. I wouldn't take it seriously enough and I wouldn't be prepared. I might say the wrong thing or be too casual.

T: So, are you saying anxiety *can* be a good thing?

P: I guess, *sometimes*.

T: So, what is the purpose of anxiety, then?

P: I guess a small amount helps you cope with situations.

T: Right. In fact, the purpose of anxiety is to protect you from danger and harm. Anxiety is an automatic response that occurs when we perceive threat. Anxiety alerts us and helps us prepare to take action if necessary. But, it's a response to *perceived* threat; which means that actual danger doesn't need to be present. Sometimes we interpret a situation as dangerous when the level of threat is actually low. But as long as we *perceive* threat, we will experience the anxiety. The important point here is that anxiety, in and of itself, is not abnormal or 'crazy'. It serves to protect you and is important for survival. Does this make sense?

P: I never thought of it that way; but I see what you mean.

Next, ask the patient to identify what happens when he or she (or anyone, for that matter) feels anxious, nervous, stressed, or frightened. Write the responses on a whiteboard or easel and arrange them in columns of physiological, cognitive, and behavioral responses as shown in Table 10. If the patient cannot come up with examples for each of the columns, provide hints (e.g., "What happens to your breathing?"). Once the patient has identified the various components of anxiety, normalize and explain the phenomena present in each component by reviewing the material in the Fight-or-Flight Response handout (Appendix 5). Give the patient a copy of the handout, which also debunks common misinter-

Table 10
Symptoms of Anxiety Typically Identified by Patients

– Racing/pounding heart	– Racing thoughts	– Avoidance of the danger
– Sweating	– Preoccupation	– Escape/get away from threat
– Heavy breathing	– Thinking the worst	– Restlessness
– Difficulty catching breath	– Trouble concentrating	– Fidgeting
– Nausea		
– Diarrhea		
– Lightheaded/dizzy		
– Muscle tension		
– Shaking/trembling		
– Hot flash		
– Cold/shivering		

pretations of fight-or-flight-related symptoms. It is important for patients to have a working knowledge of this information; and because the handout covers a large amount of material, patients should be asked to read the handout daily and to note any questions that come to mind so they can be addressed at the next session.

Threatening Thoughts and Their Effects

Explaining the role of maladaptive thinking patterns in health anxiety

This educational module focuses first on the distinction between *physical symptoms* and the *meanings* or interpretations ascribed to them, which many patients overlook. Next, it covers the relationship between appraisals of threat and emotional and behavioral responses.

Body Sensations and Threatening Interpretations. Give the patient the Body Symptom Handout (Appendix 6), which includes space for listing troublesome body sensations and how they are appraised. The patient records recent body sensations on the form and then is asked to reiterate the threatening thoughts that come to mind when these symptoms are noticed (e.g., "feeling weak means I have MS"). These appraisals are not challenged at this point; rather the therapist is simply assessing which cognitions are present. This form serves as the basis for the upcoming discussion about how thoughts influence emotions and behaviors.

Threatening Thoughts Affect How We Feel and What We Do. The idea that our emotions and behaviors are determined by our *beliefs and perceptions* of situations (and not by the situations themselves) is the basis of CBT (Beck, 1976). Patients must understand the process by which their beliefs and interpretations lead to emotional responses. Specifically, when we hold beliefs and interpretations that exaggerate threat, it makes us feel anxious, fearful and worried.

Threatening thinking occurs on two levels. **Automatic thoughts** are in-situation appraisals that go through a person's mind and provoke anxiety and the urge to seek reassurance or remove the threat. For example, when someone with a fear of brain tumors gets a headache, he or she might think, "I'm dying of brain cancer." **Dysfunctional assumptions**, on the other hand, are general underlying beliefs that people hold about themselves and the world which make them inclined to interpret specific situations and stimuli in a threatening manner. For example, the beliefs "I am highly susceptible to illness" and "My doctors can't figure out what is wrong with me" would evoke distress and urges to check and seek reassurance if an unexplained or unexpected bodily sensation was noticed.

The vignette below illustrates the use of Socratic dialogue to help a patient understand how her thinking dictates her emotional and behavioral responses:

> T: Suppose you and a friend plan to meet for dinner at 7:00 and it is now 7:30 and your friend hasn't shown up or even called to say that she'll be late. If you conclude that your friend decided that she doesn't like you anymore and therefore that you're a loser, how will you feel?
>
> P: Sad or depressed.
>
> T: Right. How about if you believed your friend was being late on purpose just to jerk your chain?
>
> P: Then I'd feel angry.

T: Sure. How about if you thought that your friend had been in a terrible accident?

P: I'd be worried.

T: Exactly. Do you see the importance of your thinking?

P: Yes. Depending on how I interpret the same situation, I could feel different emotions.

T: That's right. The way you think about situations influences your emotional responses. So, <u>you</u>, not situations, have control over your emotions.

After illustrating this model using a situation that is not emotionally charged, the next step is to apply it to a situation related to heath anxiety. The patient in the example below had an excessive fear of skin cancer.

T: Now, let's see how this might apply to your health concerns. You wrote down that when you notice a blemish on your skin, you interpret it as meaning that you have a melanoma and need to get help right away. What kinds of feelings do you think these sorts of thoughts provoke?

P: I feel scared of course.

T: Right. Anyone who thinks they have cancer would feel worried and would ask for reassurance to make sure they are OK. So, it's not surprising that when you think about your body symptoms this way it makes you feel scared, and it makes you call your doctor, ask your family what they think, or find information on the computer to make you feel better. Do you see how your interpretation of your skin blemish as being very threatening leads you to get emotional and to try to get reassurance about it?

P: Yes, but I really think I'm getting cancer at that moment.

T: Sure. Today, we're not deciding whether you are right or wrong. Your feelings and emotions are probably very strong because you really believe this threatening thought – whether true or not. Do you understand what I mean?

Safety Behaviors and Their Effects

The first aim of this educational module is to teach the patient how safety behaviors such as checking, reassurance-seeking, avoidance, searching the internet, and other subtle safety behaviors and signals grow into excessive and maladaptive patterns in time. The following points are important to convey:

Explaining the role of excessive behaviors

- It makes sense that if you are worried about your health and safety, you should check to make sure the situation is safe, that you are OK, or look for ways to feel better or safer. The things we do to make us feel safer are called "safety behaviors." Some safety behaviors make good sense, such as buckling your seat belt when you get into an automobile.
- When people have problems with unexplained physical symptoms, they may use safety behaviors because they feel like something bad, such as a serious medical condition, could happen. Naturally, these safety behaviors are connected to a specific symptom or a particular threatening thought or idea. For example, if you feel like your throat is closing in and you think, "I'm going to suffocate," a safety behavior might be to take a drink of water to check that you can still swallow correctly.

- Ask the patient to identify some examples of his or her own safety behaviors.
- Safety behaviors can lead to feeling better. They might reduce a symptom, give you reassurance, or help you avoid a feared situation. But the feeling of relief is usually only temporary. Then, the body symptom or the health concerns come back, leading only to more and more safety behaviors.
- Another problem with safety behaviors is that they tend to get more intense over time. Initially, only one or two brief safety behaviors are used. As concerns with unexplained symptoms progress, however, the person ends up spending more and more time engaged in fruitless safety behaviors (so that day-to-day functioning becomes impaired).

Next, discuss how the excessive use of safety behaviors maintains health anxiety and can even exacerbate bodily symptoms. Convey the following key points:

- When someone gets carried away with using safety behaviors in response to unexplained bodily symptoms, a number of problems can develop.
- Many safety behaviors increase awareness of body sensations. For example, body checking encourages preoccupation with the very body sensations that trigger health concerns. Seeking reassurance from doctors, relatives, or the Internet leads to an increased focus on body sensations. This increased attention leads to noticing more sensations that could seem serious, even if they are not.
- Safety behaviors can seem to verify concerns about health. If body checking, for example, leads to detecting an ambiguous bodily sign (e.g., a change in the consistency of one's feces) that may be due to normal factors (e.g., changes in diet), it may appear that a serious medical

Clinical Pearl
Integrating Psychoeducation into the Functional Assessment

A useful way to think about the initial sessions of CBT is as an exchange of information between patient and therapist. On the one hand, the patient is an "expert" on his or her particular health anxiety symptoms and must help the therapist understand the nuances of these symptoms in order for an individual treatment plan to be developed. On the other hand, the therapist is an expert in conceptualizing health anxiety symptoms and must teach the patient to understand his or her symptoms in a way that best fosters benefit from the treatment procedures.

In our clinic, we explain this situation to patients at the very beginning of the functional assessment phase. We weave the psychoeducational component into this assessment by capitalizing on any opportunities to help the patient understand the functional aspects of his or her symptoms. For example, when assessing automatic thoughts associated with physical symptoms, if a patient describes these thoughts and physical symptoms as "abnormal" or potential signs of a serious medical illness (in the absence of any medical evidence), we begin educating him or her immediately about the normalcy of body noise. This technique helps socialize the patient to the biopsychosocial model of health anxiety, which is critical for a positive treatment response.

condition is present. Indeed, some patients report a temporary *increase* in anxiety after body checking.

- Reassurance-seeking can reinforce threatening thinking. If a doctor prescribes another test "just to be on the safe side," or when multiple consultations result in conflicting information, it can lead to greater uncertainty and worry.
- Finally, using safety behaviors, cues, and avoidance prevents the person from having opportunities to disconfirm their threatening health-related beliefs and interpretations.

4.1.4   Cognitive Therapy Techniques

Cognitive therapy techniques for health anxiety teach patients to identify, challenge, and modify dysfunctional thinking patterns (i.e., maladaptive assumptions and interpretations) that give rise to extreme health worries and checking, avoidance, reassurance-seeking, and safety behaviors and signals. The focus specifically relies on collecting evidence that is *inconsistent* with the patient's disease convictions and *consistent* with the biopsychosocial model. This evidence may be examined through verbal discussion, or using "behavioral experiments" designed to test the logic of certain beliefs.

How to use cognitive therapy techniques for health anxiety

For some patients, health anxiety is focused on specific and immediate concerns (e.g., heart failure, stroke) which may be possible to disconfirm by exploring the relevant facts. Other patients, however, worry about progressive or long-term negative outcomes (e.g., cancer, multiple sclerosis). While it may be impossible to disconfirm that such diseases *might* develop *in the future*, cognitive techniques can focus on possible alternative explanations and outcomes.

Discussing and Challenging Cognitive Distortions

Identifying patterns of thoughts and beliefs about body symptoms and general health issues raises awareness of how such thinking patterns lead to health worries. Promote **collaborative empiricism** by asking questions to help the patient discover for him or herself an understanding of how maladaptive thinking patterns contribute to their problems with health worries. Appendix 7 provides a list of common maladaptive thinking patterns in health anxiety. Review this handout in the session and explore with the patient how such thinking styles might play a role in his or her particular complaints. The text below describes how to help patients challenge these maladaptive patterns. Detailed descriptions and illustrative case examples of these techniques can be found in our comprehensive textbook on the treatment of health anxiety (Abramowitz & Braddock, 2008).

Helping the patient challenge maladaptive thinking patterns

All-or-Nothing Thinking. The most common manifestations of this thinking style are beliefs such as "good health means being 100 % symptom-free all of the time," and that "any bodily symptom is always a sign of a physical illness." Of course, this perspective overlooks the normalcy of body noise, the fight-or-flight response, and other benign sensations and body variations.

One strategy for challenging all-or-nothing thinking is to review the concepts of homeostasis, body noise, the physical response to health anxiety, and how the mind and body influence one another. You might discuss how psychological stress can induce symptoms such as headaches and asthma. Patients can list examples of their own worrisome body sensations and consider the evidence for and against their belief that these are signs of a medical condition.

Additionally, it might be helpful to explore the advantages and disadvantages of this type of thinking. *Advantages* include that this is a convenient way to view the world and make sense of one's health. It also reduces the chance of overlooking a serious problem if one happens to be present. The major *disadvantage* is that all-or-nothing thinking leads to repeated "false alarms" in which benign body sensations are mistaken for medical symptoms. This leads to worrying, unnecessary doctor visits, strained relations with relatives and medical professionals, frequent body checking, and other maladaptive behaviors (e.g., reassurance-seeking), which maintain the problem.

The following behavioral experiments may also be useful in addressing all-or-nothing thinking:

- In the "Rumination Experiment," the patient worries aloud for several minutes about an actual predicament unrelated to health anxiety). This reliably evokes changes in mood and increased physical arousal (i.e., bodily changes). You can then discuss with the patient how worrying affects the body and whether the body sensations that occurred during the experiment were more likely related to worrying or to a suddenly occurring medical illness.

- The "No Help" experiment targets the belief, "If I don't get to a doctor at the first sign of trouble, I will develop a serious illness." The patient is instructed to postpone health-related visits and phone calls to doctors and relatives. Most patients predict that they will not be able to stop obsessing about what might be wrong with them. This prediction can be tested by monitoring daily levels of health anxiety and preoccupation with symptoms each day between sessions. Most patients find that they do not remain preoccupied, and that the symptoms bother them less and less as time passes. At the subsequent sessions, process the outcome of the experiment and generate more healthy cognitions such as, "My symptoms will eventually fade even if I do not visit or call the doctor."

Fortune-Telling. The most helpful way to challenge this pattern is to help the patient consider evidence for and against their predictions. Laura, for example, believed her circulatory system was weak. She thought that if she elevated her head when she slept (i.e., by using a pillow), she would die since too little blood would get to her brain. Laura even had a bed that tilted so her head was *below* her heart when she slept. Laura's therapist helped her challenge these beliefs using the following verbal techniques:

- Laura was asked to clarify specifically what the nature of her illness was, and exactly how it would kill her. When she was unable to produce a logical "story," the therapist helped Laura understand that her beliefs had gotten the best of her and that she had no logical basis for them.

- Laura was asked to examine the evidence for and against her health concerns. Very little evidence supported her belief; however, she disqualified all of the evidence that did not support the belief. For example, when the therapist pointed out that Laura seemed to have no circulatory difficulties when sitting up and standing, she argued that her heart and blood vessels worked more efficiently when she was awake than when sleeping. When questioned about the basis for this assumption, Laura could not identify any valid source. The therapist helped Laura to see how she was discounting information merely because it did not support her belief, rather than based on its validity.

- Keeping in mind that her predictions *might* be incorrect, Laura was asked to identify the advantages and disadvantages of holding them. An advantage was that it *could* be a matter of life and death. Disadvantages included that it evoked anxiety, strange sleeping habits, constant preoccupation and monitoring her body, and that it led to poor relationships with her physicians.

Behavioral experiments for challenging fortune telling beliefs usually involve ceasing avoidance and safety behaviors to find out whether the threatening predictions are realistic. Laura and her therapist, for example, decided to conduct a test of Laura's beliefs about dying in her sleep. This involved Laura gradually decreasing the tilt of her bed each night until it was horizontal. Then, a pillow was added to elevate her head.

Negative Interpretations. Strategies for challenging negative interpretations of bodily signs and sensations include examining evidence for and against the faulty appraisals, and considering *all* of the evidence, rather than only that which seems to confirm the fear-related interpretation (see *disqualifying* further below). Reviewing psychoeducational modules about body noise and benign explanations for noticeable sensations and perturbations provides a basis for identifying less threatening explanations (e.g., "Based on what you have learned, what other explanations could there be?"). Alternative explanations can be tested out in behavioral experiments.

A particularly useful behavioral experiment involves inducing feared bodily sensations using exaggerations of everyday behaviors as displayed in Table 11. Both the therapist and patient should perform these procedures and then compare notes to help the patient see that even healthy people (e.g., the therapist) can experience uncomfortable body sensations. Further, a discussion of how these sensations are produced by fairly routine activities provides a nonthreatening interpretation for the feared sensations (e.g., "If getting up from lying down can causes me to feel dizzy, maybe that explains why I worry I am having a stroke every morning when I get out of bed").

Another experiment is to have the patient switch between "body *focusing*" and "*non-focusing*" days. On focusing days, the patient pays constant attention and closely monitors feared body sensations. He or she also is allowed to engage in body-checking and reassurance-seeking. On non-focusing days, no monitoring, checking or reassurance-seeking is allowed. The patient monitors daily levels of anxiety, body sensations, urges to check and seek assurances, and the strength of belief in the negative interpretation using a scale from 0% to 100%. The alternating days continue for a week or two so that consistent results can be obtained. Most patients report that, to their surprise, non-focusing days are easier than focusing days. These results can be discussed within the context of the biopsychosocial model. Importantly, this experiment should be carried out during a relatively typical period of time for the patient, *and when no doctor visits are planned*, since these can increase body noise and confound the experiment.

Table 11
Procedures for Inducing Feared Body Sensations

Body sensation	Suggested procedures
Racing heart	• Jog in place • Walk/run up and down flights of stairs
Dizziness	• Place head between legs • Hyperventilate (60-90 seconds) • Spin head back and forth • Rapidly get up from a prone or sitting position
Throat sensations	• Tighten a neck tie • Try to quickly swallow 5 times in a row
Pain	• Hold arms in the air (with weights) for extended period of time • Tense muscles
Gag response	• Brush back of the tongue with a toothbrush
Suffocation	• Hold breath • Breath through a straw
Sweating, flushing	• Jog in place • Walk/run up and down flights of stairs

People with health anxiety focus on the *possibilities* rather than the *probabilities*

Intolerance of Uncertainty. Intolerance of uncertainty is central to the experience of health anxiety. Many patients consider the *possibility* of an illness as implying that the illness is *probable*, which leads to the urge to obtain a logically impossible absolute 100% guarantee of good health or perfect explanation for their symptoms. People without health anxiety, on the other hand, are able to *feel* confident about their health despite the fact that absolute certainty is more or less an illusion. The following demonstration can be used to illustrate the ubiquity of uncertainty in everyday life.

T: Your husband dropped you off at the session today, right?

P: Yes. His name is Noah.

T: Great. Is Noah alive right now; at this very moment?

P: Sure. Why do you ask?

T: Well, I am interested in how you know *for sure* that he's alive.

P: Like you said, he dropped me off.

T: But that was about half an hour ago, right? Isn't it possible that something terrible happened to him just in the last half-hour? You never know what *could* happen, do you?

P: I guess that's true. So, I guess I don't know for *certain* that he's alive. But, I would bet that he is.

This can lead to a discussion of how the patient coped in a healthy way with uncertainty about her spouse, basing her judgment on probability (i.e., a *guess*), as opposed to needing to be absolutely certain. Other low probability events the patient takes for granted on a regular basis can also be discussed, such as using scissors and electrical appliances (potential sources of injury), crossing the street, and even driving to the therapy session (potentially deadly). This helps patients understand that they already know how to manage uncertainty. Therefore, they can learn how to tolerate other low-risk uncertainties, such as those associated with their health concerns.

The following is a continuation of the dialogue from further above. This patient's health anxiety concerns the unfounded fear of a ruptured spleen.

T: So, you said that although you don't know for certain that Noah is alive right now, you'd still *bet* that he is. What kind of a bet are you making when you feel a pain in your stomach and you think it feels like your spleen is ruptured?

P: I'm betting it means my spleen is ruptured but the doctors don't notice it.

T: Right, and where does that bet lead you?

P: I see what you mean. I get frantic and start calling doctors and looking online for information and reassurance.

T: Yeah, and what do all of the doctors tell you?

P: Well, they *say* I'm fine. But I *could* have a ruptured spleen. It really feels like it's ruptured. My doctors *could* be wrong.

T: You're right. They could be. But, remember, Noah *could* be dead right now and you *could* be in an accident driving home from our session today. Do you think you could apply the same logic to your spleen concerns that you use when you think about Noah and driving?

P: I guess so. Just like with Noah probably being alive right now, I *probably* don't have a spleen problem.

Clinical Pearl
Fears of Illnesses in the Distant Future

Some patients describe concerns about future medical problems, or those with long-term or slow onsets (e.g., a slowly progressing rare brain illness, insidious cancer). Here, it is fruitless to use cognitive therapy to try to convince patients that the feared illness will *never* occur. Indeed, even the most knowledgeable physician cannot guarantee such things. Moreover, trying to derive reassuring "evidence" would merely be helping the patient seek reassurance about something that no one can be reassured of completely. The patient will eventually find reasons why this guarantee is not sufficient (physicians sometimes fall into this trap when consulting with health-anxious individuals). The most helpful approach here is first, to acknowledge that a definitive guarantee or explanation is not possible. Next, help the patient generate a less threatening interpretation of the uncertainty (e.g., "Most people experience body symptoms they can't explain" or "No one really knows what will happen to them when they get older; no one can really predict the future"). Thus, the goal becomes learning to accept reasonable, everyday levels of uncertainty that everyone faces in life.

Once the patient is willing to accept uncertainty, additional cognitive therapy and exposure exercises (described later in this chapter) can be used to teach the patient that uncertainty is manageable.

Salkovskis, Warwick, and Deale (2003) describe the following behavioral experiment to illustrate the futility of reassurance-seeking. First, agree to offer the patient a session in which you will focus on providing unlimited reassurance – for example, attempting to answer all questions and collect as much information as they would like – regarding their feared illness. Next, collect information, review medical records, have a conference call with the physician (do whatever it takes) until the patient feels at least somewhat reassured for the time being. Then, at a subsequent session, assess how successful the reassurance was at reducing his/her anxiety. For most patients, the effects are short-lived; and the reasons for this can be explored.

It is useful to examine the short and long-term advantages and disadvantages of learning to live with uncertainty versus trying to seek guarantees. Note the example in Figure 3, which shows that the advantages of living with uncertainty are *long-term*, while the disadvantages are primarily *short-term*. The opposite is true for trying to obtain a guarantee. Explain that people generally take the quickest path to relief. Thus, reassurance-seeking makes sense as a short-term coping strategy, but it leads to trouble in the long-term. The patient can keep a list of these advantages and disadvantages to refer to when the urge to seek reassurance arises.

The patient can also identify people that he or she asks for reassurance (e.g., a partner/spouse, parent), and invite them to attend a therapy session to learn about the maladaptive effects of providing reassurance. Physicians who offer assurances can also be included (e.g., via a conference call). During the session, explain how these individuals can help by not giving in to requests for reassurance. Appendix 8 includes possible responses others can use when the patient engages in reassurance-seeking. Situations can be role played to ensure that these situations are dealt with constructively.

| | Living with Uncertainty About my Health | |
	Short-term	Long-term
Disadvantages	• Might be sick and not know it • More anxiety and worry • I'd be irritable and preoccupied • Less productivity • It's very difficult	• Might not know if I was sick until it's too late
Advantages		• Feeling at peace with my body • No more body checking • Better relationships with doctors • Notice less symptoms • Better able to accept what doctors are telling me • Less preoccupation • Better work and home functioning

Figure 3
Short- and long-term advantages and disadvantages of tolerating uncertainty and of seeking reassurance

Assumptions About Probability, Severity, and Inability to Cope. This type of cognitive distortion is characterized by overestimates of the *probability* of harm ("jumping to conclusions") and overestimation of *severity* ("catastrophizing"). Many patients assume (without any evidence on which to base their assumption) that they could not cope if a serious illness were to befall them. Such beliefs lead to feeling that intolerable illnesses are omnipresent, which leads to increased anxiety, vigilance and misinterpreting ostensibly harmless bodily sensations.

Health anxious patients often acknowledge that a feared illness is *unlikely*. Yet, because the perceived *severity* of having the illness is high (e.g., "it *could* be fatal"), they engage in avoidance, reassurance-seeking, checking, and other safety behaviors. Such thinking and behavior indicates the failure to separate the *costs* of a medical problem from its *probability*, which can be addressed in cognitive therapy through the use of Socratic questioning. Patients may believe they narrowly escape tragedy because of their avoidance and reliance on safety behaviors and signals. Here, it may be helpful to review how avoidance and safety behaviors maintain problematic thinking patterns.

Finally, it might be helpful to discuss the reality that sooner or later, almost everyone develops an illness of one sort or another – perhaps even a life-threatening condition. But, that most people cope with such circumstances better than they might imagine. The therapist might ask the patient to conduct interviews with people who have suffered serious illnesses to gain insight into the strategies and thought processes that were used to cope. In session, Socratic questions can be used to help the patient build self-efficacy for coping with serious illnesses if and when they occur.

Disqualifying. Health anxious individuals may selectively accept evidence that seemingly confirms the presence of an illness and reject or discount that which does not. As a result, it may be difficult to rationally discuss their health concerns.

The "Pie Chart Technique" helps patients increase their range of nonthreatening explanations for innocuous body sensations. This involves asking the patient to identify a worrisome body sensation (e.g., headache). Next, all the *possible* causes of this sensation are listed (e.g., eye strain, muscle tension, stress, etc.), *including the patient's threatening interpretations* (e.g., brain tumor). Then, the patient estimates the percentage of headaches attributable to each possible cause and constructs a pie graph of this information. The patient next further divides the slice representing his or her threatening interpretation into two slices to account for (a) people (like the patient) who have had negative tests for the feared illness, and (b) those who have had positive tests. This technique illustrates, and can lead to a discussion of, how the patient might selectively focus on certain health information.

Additionally, patients can be instructed to survey others about their body sensations and health-related experiences. For example, they can ask 10 people whether they also believe that "doctors are likely to miss the tell-tale signs and symptoms of serious illnesses when they evaluate patients." The results of the survey can be discussed in session to help the patient consider alternate perspectives. If the patient discounts evidence gained through these behavioral experiments (e.g., "people who took the poll are different from me"), the therapist can ask how many more people would have to be polled before he or she would consider the results valid. This can highlight the excessiveness of the patient's belief. For example, if a patient says "everyone would need to disagree with my belief in order to convince me that I am wrong," it can be pointed out that the patient's beliefs are different from "everyone" else's.

Holding Lofty Standards. Extremely high expectations of medical professionals (e.g., "Doctors should be able to explain everything that's wrong with me") indicates a failure to grasp key concepts covered in the psychoeducation modules. Therefore, it may be helpful to review these and discuss how even the most well-trained and experienced physician cannot possibly explain every bodily sensation.

As a behavioral experiment, the patient can delay acting on urges to seek medical consultation and other forms of reassurance after noticing a bodily sensation. The delay period might be several days to a week, and the patient should keep a calendar and notes during this time. If the feared body sensations are still present after the experiment, he or she may then consult a physician. Most patients report that the feared "symptoms" subside by the time the delay period ends, and this can be used as evidence that the physician's assessment is probably correct.

Some health anxious individuals "over-inform" their providers based on the idea that medical providers are incompetent. If a medical visit has been scheduled for the near future, a behavioral experiment can involve the patient deliberately leaving out details he or she fears might result in a mistake. Usually, the patient finds that the physician ends up asking questions that elicit this information. Patients may also feel they are being taken seriously and that their patient-doctor relationship is strong. Some patients even find themselves listening more closely and learning from the physician, rather than worrying whether they have described their symptoms sufficiently to avoid a catastrophe.

Intolerance of Anxiety. Beliefs that it is dangerous to be anxious (e.g., anxiety will persist forever, spiral to unmanageable levels, and cause serious physical harm) render the individual hypervigilant to the sensations associated with normal physiological arousal (i.e., fight-or-flight). This, in turn, leads to noticing more body sensations, which reinforces beliefs that something is medically wrong. When this thinking pattern is present, therapists should review the psychoeducational modules regarding body noise and the fight-or-flight response. Myths and misinterpretations about the harmful effects of anxiety can be addressed by assessing catastrophic beliefs about harm from long-term

---

Clinical Pearl
Capitalizing on Opportunities to Maximize Cognitive Change

Cognitive techniques should be used liberally throughout CBT for health anxiety. The following are a few examples of how these strategies can be applied at various points:

- During exposure exercises (described later in this chapter), help the patient process his or her experience. Review evidence regarding the probability and severity of actually being ill. Help the patient articulate more realistic beliefs about the physical sensations he or she misinterprets.
- Identify and summarize changes in beliefs during and after the completion of exposure exercises. Once the patient is socialized to the biopsychosocial model, ask *him or her* to provide such summaries.
- If self-monitoring forms indicate persistent health concerns, help the patient identify underlying dysfunctional cognitions. For example, "What were you saying to yourself when you noticed that your leg felt weak?" and "What were the short- and long-term consequences of calling your doctor to ask about that?"

---

anxiety and by providing corrective information through didactic and Socratic discussion. For example, the patient can describe previous experiences with anxiety to illustrate that such sensations subside over time and are not harmful.

4.1.5 Exposure and Response Prevention

The aim of exposure and response prevention is to provide experiences in which the patient confronts feared stimuli (exposure) without any checking or reassurance-seeking, or safety behaviors or signals (response prevention). Prolonged exposure initially provokes an increase in subjective anxiety, followed by a natural (and gradual) decline in this distress. The **fear hierarchy** is a list of the health anxiety triggers (situations, stimuli, bodily sensations) that the patient confronts during exposure exercises. Hierarchy items are ranked according to the level of distress that the patient expects to encounter during exposure to that particular item.

Exposure and response prevention are very powerful in producing changes in maladaptive cognitions

Explaining Exposure and Response Prevention

It is important to provide a rationale for the use of exposure therapy since it often seems anxiety provoking (and therefore contradictary) to patients. The following points should be discussed:

The patient must understand the rationale for using exposure therapy

- The treatment techniques, **exposure** and **response prevention**, are designed to weaken maladaptive thinking and behavior patterns in people with health anxiety and worry.
- Exposure involves gradually confronting the situations and provoking the bodily sensations that provoke anxiety. Response prevention involves resisting the urge to check, seek reassurance, or do anything to escape from the distress, except enduring the feared situation.
- Give examples of specific exposure and response prevention exercises that might be prescribed for the patient.

- The basic idea of exposure therapy is simple. Repeatedly confronting anxiety-provoking situations and deliberately inducing anxiety-provoking bodily sensations so that they may be systematically confronted helps the patient learn that anxiety does not remain at high levels or spiral "out of control." Instead, distress actually subsides on its own; a process known as **habituation**. Since the patient usually escapes from the feared situation before anxiety subsides through checking or engaging in safety behaviors, he or she does not usually have the opportunity to see that habituation eventually occurs. In short, exposure weakens the connections between feared situations, body sensations, and anxiety.
- Exposure also helps patients learn to more effectively manage normal, everyday levels of uncertainty about health and illness

Draw for the patient a graph similar to that in Figure 4 to depict the within- and between-session habituation curves over the course of several exposure sessions. Discuss the graph as follows:

Explaining the procedures of exposure therapy

- The patient should expect to feel anxious during exposure, especially when starting to confront the feared situation. But this distress is temporary; it eventually subsides if the patient remains in the feared situation.
- The graph illustrates what happens with repeated and prolonged exposure. In the beginning of the first session, discomfort increases and then declines as time passes. At the second session, the discomfort subsides more quickly because learning has occurred. After several exposure trials, the initial distress level is lower and it subsides even more quickly. With repeated practice, the feared situations no longer provoke anxiety.
- This pattern only occurs if the exposure exercise is carefully designed and if the patient remains exposed for an extended period of time without escaping or seeking reassurance (i.e., the patient must "invest anxiety now in order to have a calmer future").

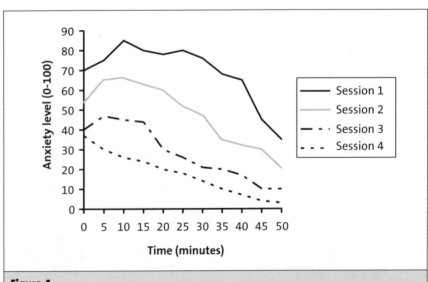

Figure 4
Expected pattern of within-session and between-sessions habituation during repeated exposure

- Two kinds of exposure are used in the treatment of health anxiety: **Situational** (or **in vivo**) exposure involves facing the actual feared situations. **Interoceptive** exposure involves purposely inducing feared body sensations so the patient may systematically confront them in therapy.
- The therapist and patient will construct a list of exposure stimuli to be ordered from the least to most anxiety-provoking.
- All exposure exercises will be planned ahead of time (collaboratively) to avoid surprises.
- The therapist will provide support and coaching during each exposure task, but will not force the patient into exposure tasks. The patient must *choose* exposure instead of avoidance and instead of the use of anxiety-reduction strategies.
- The patient must prepare to "tough it out" when the going gets rough. This may be challenging in the beginning, but it will get easier.

Situational Exposure

Building the Situational Hierarchy. Compose two lists, based on the results of the functional assessment, and with the patient's assistance. Include the situations in the first list and the bodily sensations that trigger excessive health concerns, or that the patient avoids, in the second. Record these situations and sensations on the Exposure Hierarchy Form (Appendix 9). The following are examples of situations and stimuli that often appear on situational exposure hierarchies for health anxiety. (An example of a fear hierarchy appears in the case vignette presented in Chapter 5.) Remember that your patient's hierarchy will be specific to his or her particular feared situations, stimuli, and body sensations.

Situational or *in vivo* exposure means confronting real life stimuli

- Reading books and articles about the feared illness (e.g., a patient who believes he has ALS could read the book *Tuesdays with Morrie*)
- Talking with someone who has the feared illness (e.g., a cancer patient)
- Watching a television show, movie, or play about someone suffering from the feared illness
- Reading news stories warning about health threats
- Visiting a local hospital or sitting in a clinic waiting room
- Attending funerals or visiting a funeral home or cemetery
- Reading the obituary section of the newspaper
- Writing one's own obituary
- Going to the doctor for a check-up, or giving oneself a breast or testicular exam (only for someone who *avoids* such activities)
- Going into buildings that the patient erroneously associates with asbestos (e.g., perhaps asbestos was found there some time ago)
- Visiting the place where a friend or family member died

The most therapeutic exposures are those which allow patients to test (and disconfirm) their health-related fears (e.g., "I will get sick just by being in a hospital"). However, in some instances the fears pertain to the distant future (e.g., "I will get cancer in 40 years from being around fluorescent light bulbs"). In such cases, exposure tasks should be designed with the understanding that the goal is to learn to tolerate acceptable levels of uncertainty.

What makes an exposure exercise effective?

Once an initial list of items is generated, ask the patient to assign a numerical rating of subjective units of distress ("SUDS") for each item (i.e., "How anxious would you feel if you confronted _____?"). The SUDS scale includes a range from 0 (no distress) to 100 (maximal distress), although it can be introduced using the anchors shown in the box below. Record the patient's SUDS ratings on the fear hierarchy form.

Explaining Subjective Units of Distress

The Subjective Units of Distress (SUDS) Scale
- 0 SUDS = no distress (like you are asleep).
- 25 SUDS = minimal distress.
- 50 SUDS = moderate distress.
- 75 SUDS = high distress.
- 100 SUDS = maximum distress (e.g., being tied to the railroad tracks as the train is coming around the bend).

Next, working with the patient, establish the order in which hierarchy items will be confronted (and record this on the hierarchy form). Some considerations for designing this treatment plan are as follows:
- Begin with moderately distressing items (e.g., 40 SUDS) and gradually work up to the most disturbing items.
- Items that were inadvertently omitted from the hierarchy can always be added after discussion with the patient.
- When possible, each item is first confronted under the therapist's supervision and then practiced between sessions.

How to conduct situational exposure

Conducting Situational Exposure. Each exposure session is planned in advance. The patient confronts the predetermined hierarchy item(s) and remains exposed until the level of distress dissipates. No reassurance-seeking, checking, or safety behaviors and signals are permitted (see Response Prevention section later in this chapter). Exposure trials may last from 15 to 90 minutes depending on the patient's fear response and pattern of habituation. The therapist asks for a rating of SUDS levels every five minutes through the exercise; the exercise ends when distress is minimal (or at least at 50-60 % reduction in SUDS).

Begin each exposure session by providing the patient with the specifics of the planned exercise (e.g., how and where the feared stimulus will be confronted, how long it will last, which anxiety-reducing behaviors are not permitted). During early exposure sessions review the 10 Tips for Successful Exposure handout (see Appendix 10) to give the patient a better idea of how the exercise is to proceed. A brief description of the exercise and an initial SUDS rating should be entered on the Exposure Practice Form (Appendix 11), which is used to keep track of progress during each exercise.

How to introduce an exposure exercise

The following is a representative introduction to a situational exposure task for a patient preoccupied and fearful of developing glaucoma:

    T: At our last meeting we agreed that for today's exposure session you would practice reading stories about glaucoma. So, I brought a handful of personal stories from glaucoma sufferers that I found on the Internet, stories from loved ones of sufferers, and some scientific articles about glaucoma. We can begin with whichever you think would be the least distressing to read. By the end of the session I'd like you to read all of these and then plan to write a story about *yourself* having glaucoma for homework practice. Does that sound OK?

P: Well, it sounds like it will be tough, but I know it's what I have to do.

T: That's the spirit! Now, while you read these stories, it's important that you allow yourself to focus on any disturbing thoughts that may come to mind. I don't want you to push your worries away. Just let yourself worry about glaucoma; let those kinds of thoughts just 'hang out' in your mind. Also remember that you are going to practice not checking your eyes and you must not go for any ophthalmology exams this week, OK?

P: Yes, I understand.

T: Good. I know this is going to produce anxiety for you, but doing this exposure will help teach you how to successfully manage thoughts and reminders of glaucoma that you have been going out of your way to avoid. You will see that your distress will subside if you confront these things and allow yourself to become anxious. I will be keeping track of your anxiety level during the exposure by asking you to rate your SUDS level every five minutes. Are you ready to start?

Troubleshooting. For many patients, success with early exposure exercises predicts success with later, more challenging ones. If the patient struggles with the early exercises, however, convey sensitivity and understanding that such tasks are highly distressing. Reiterate that this distress, however, is temporary. The following strategies are helpful:

- Model the task prior to instructing the patient to engage.
- Use cognitive therapy techniques to identify and modify dysfunctional beliefs that evoke high anxiety or prevent the patient from agreeing to engage in exposures.
- If applicable, discuss how cognitive change and anxiety reduction have occurred during previous exposures.
- Discuss the importance of learning to take acceptable risks.
- Revisit the importance of learning to tolerate uncertainty.
- Provide praise for successfully completing exposure tasks.

Interoceptive Exposure

Systematic exposure to bodily sensations that provoke anxiety (i.e., **interoceptive exposure**), was developed by Barlow and colleagues (e.g., Barlow, Craske, Cerny, & Klosko, 1989) to help patients with panic disorder face feared arousal-related internal sensations (e.g., dizziness). The procedure involves intentionally re-creating the feared body sensations (e.g., spinning to create dizziness) and allowing the patient to learn that (a) these sensations are not dangerous and, (b) the sensations and associated anxiety decline over time in the absence of any safety behaviors.

Interoceptive exposure means confronting feared bodily stimuli

Providing a Rationale. Begin with a clear explanation of interoceptive exposure since this technique sometimes seems counterproductive to patients. Keep in mind that interoceptive exposure to feared body sensations is analogous to situational exposure to feared external stimuli. The following is a script for how to introduce this technique:

T: As we have been discussing, there are certain body sensations that trigger excessive levels of anxiety for you. While these body sensations are *quite real* – you're not making them up – all of the available evidence suggests that they do not mean what you think they mean. That is, they don't seem to be a sign of any medical illness. So, it is as if you are frightened that a big tiger is waiting for you around the corner, when it is really only a kitten. The approach we use to weaken excessive anxiety that is associated with body sensations is to help you confront the sensations in a structured way. When you repeatedly confront these feelings without escaping or seeking reassurance about them, you will learn that you are able to control and reduce the feared sensations more than you had thought. You will also learn that you can purposely bring these sensations on in different ways. This will help you see that there is no basis for your fears. Finally, you will learn more productive ways of responding when the sensations occur so that you do not continue to be preoccupied with your health.

Building the Interoceptive Exposure Hierarchy. As with situational exposure, a hierarchy-driven approach is recommended in which less disturbing (or less intense) sensations are confronted before the most upsetting ones. Planning for interoceptive exposure requires determining which body sensations need to be provoked and how to provoke them. Procedures for producing many commonly feared bodily signs and sensations are discussed later in this section. Items on the interoceptive hierarchy can be recorded on the Exposure Hierarchy Form (Appendix 9).

Interoceptive exposure techniques

Conducting Interoceptive Exposure. The therapist helps the patient deliberately provoke feared body sensations in the office using a variety of techniques and maneuvers. The sensation(s) is maintained or repeated without a break during the session until habituation occurs (i.e., 50% reduction in SUDS). The patient is instructed not to engage in any avoidance, checking, or reassurance-seeking behaviors that would reduce the intensity of the sensation or prevent a feared outcome (e.g., fainting). Instead, the patient is encouraged to make the sensations as intense as possible. Changes in beliefs about the dangerousness of the sensations are emphasized when discussing the outcome of the exposures.

Table 12 shows techniques for inducing commonly feared body sensations during interoceptive exposure. It is important to assess the degree to which the sensations provoked match those that the patient experiences when health anxiety concerns or panic attacks are triggered. Naturally, the particular exposure will be more effective to the extent that the provoked sensations seem realistic and similar to the actual interoceptive cues. We encourage the therapist to perform the exposure task along with the patient so that the therapist can model a calm response to the body sensations, and so that patient and therapist can compare and discuss the experience. The patient is then instructed to practice the same interoceptive exercise(s) each day between sessions. Exposure Practice Forms (Appendix 11) are used to keep track of SUDS levels both during the session and homework practice. Cognitive therapy techniques can also be used to identify and modify catastrophic beliefs about the dangerousness of the sensations.

Table 12
Techniques for Provoking Body Sensations During Interoceptive Exposure

Technique (instruction)	Body sensation(s)
Hyperventilation (rapid deep breathing for 90 seconds)	Shortness of breath, sense of unreality, tingling, sweating, dizziness, lightheadedness, dry mouth/throat, light sensitivity, chest tightness, racing heart beat, exhaustion
Body tensing (tense muscles in arms, legs, abdomen, neck, face, etc.; or do push-ups for 60 seconds)	Muscle tension, sweating, racing heart
Head lifting (place head between legs for 30 seconds, then lift head quickly to normal position; repeat)	Lightheadedness, head rush, disorientation
Swallowing (attempt to swallow 5 times in quick succession)	Throat tightness, lump in throat, breathlessness
Hold breath for as long as possible (at least 60 seconds)	Chest tightness, shortness of breath, smothering sensations
Run in place (lifting knees up to chest; or step up on stairs for 60 seconds)	Shortness of breath, racing heart beat
Stare at a small spot in the corner for 2 minutes	Sense of unreality
Spinning (either in a standing position or while seated in a revolving chair for 60 seconds)	Dizziness, disorientation
Straw breathing (breathe rapidly through a very thin straw for 60 seconds)	Shortness of breath, chest tightness, smothering sensations
Hot shower (take a hot shower with the door closed)	Weakness, disorientation, hot flash
Gag (use toothbrush to brush the back of the tongue)	Nausea
Caffeine (drink highly caffeinated beverage or take caffeine pills; e.g., NoDoz).	Racing heart, sweating, hot flash

Patients may avoid certain activities because they may provoke feared body sensations. For example, avoiding drinking caffeinated beverages because of the fear of feeling keyed up, avoiding exercise because it could strain the heart or lead to feelings of weakness, and avoiding spicy or high fiber foods because of the fear of stomach and lower GI sensations. Such situations should be included on the interoceptive or situational exposure hierarchy.

Although there is a contextual difference between the sensations provoked during interoceptive exposure (which are deliberately triggered in a therapy

Clinical Pearl
Integrating Cognitive Therapy with Exposure

Exposure therapy helps patients develop realistic estimates of the probability of feared consequences. It also helps them learn how to manage everyday uncertainty and risk surrounding personal health issues. The reduction in distress accompanying exposure helps modify dysfunctional beliefs that anxiety will persist indefinitely or spiral to harmful levels. Cognitive therapy techniques can be used at various points during exposure sessions to facilitate these cognitive changes.

- **When initiating an exposure task**, cognitive techniques can be used to identify mistaken cognitions (e.g., "I cannot bear to think about getting Alzheimer's disease") that can be tested during exposure.
- **During exposures**, cognitive techniques can be used to promote adaptive beliefs and responses to bodily sensations and health concerns (e.g., "Just because I feel uncomfortable does not mean I have a serious medical condition").
- **After an exposure exercise**, Socratic discussion – which involves asking the patient questions to help him or her to logically examine ideas – is used to review the outcome of the exercise, examine evidence for and against dysfunctional beliefs, and develop more realistic beliefs about health and illness-related stimuli. For example, ask the patient what he/she learned from the exposure exercise, or why they think their anxiety levels decreased during the exposure. This solidifies the learning process, helping to generalize an isolated exposure exercise to other experiences.

setting) and the actual sensations the cue health anxiety (which occur spontaneously and seemingly without explanation outside of therapy), interoceptive exposure can be useful to the extent that it de-catastrophizes the feared bodily sensations. Specifically, interoceptive exposure (a) teaches patients that the feared bodily sensations are temporary and manageable, and (b) provides alternative explanations for the origins of the sensations. For example, if tingling in the arms and legs can be deliberately brought on by hyperventilating in the therapist's office, then perhaps this is also causes tingling when at home. If the patient becomes concerned about such contextual differences, these points can be discussed.

Response Prevention

Response prevention is a necessary ingredient for exposure to be successful

Response prevention, which entails voluntarily refraining from reassurance-seeking and other anxiety-reducing behaviors both during and after exposure exercises, should be employed so the patient can learn that health anxiety subsides naturally, even when checking and seeking reassurance are not performed. Specific guidelines for the patient to follow should be determined collaboratively. Whereas some patients are able to immediately stop all checking, reassurance-seeking, and other safety behaviors, others require a gradual approach. Some considerations when planning for response prevention appear below.

- Revisit the psychoeducational materials presented earlier in this chapter. Discuss the negative effects of checking, reassurance-seeking, and other safety-behaviors; as well as the rationale for stopping them. Patients are often surprised at how much less attention they pay to their bodies when they do not engage in these maladaptive behaviors.

- Emphasize that refraining from these behaviors is a difficult choice.
- Define the rules for response prevention and record them on the Help with Response Prevention form (Appendix 12). Give the form to the patient as a guide.
- If relatives or friends are involved in the patient's symptoms, encourage them to help by refraining from answering reassurance-seeking questions.
- The patient is to record violations of response prevention on the Symptom Record (see Appendix 3) and bring these to the therapist so that areas in need of additional attention can be addressed. Ongoing problems with adherence to response prevention can be addressed using the trouble-shooting strategies described in Section 4.5.1 later in this chapter.

Below, we outline common response prevention plans and strategies. Note, however, that each patient will have an individualized response prevention plan.

Examples of response prevention plans for helping patients resist different types of safety behaviors

Body Checking. Patients are not to check bodily signs (e.g., pulse) or levels (blood sugar), or the skin. Inspecting or scrutinizing body fluids and excreta (aside from a simple glance) is also prohibited.

Reassurance-Seeking. Medical appointments for previously evaluated symptoms are off limits. Any "new symptoms" can be discussed with the therapist, but no doctor visits are to occur. Telephoning medical personnel or "help lines" is off limits. Internet searches for medical information are also prohibited. If the patient must be online for work or school, he or she should avoid medical websites. It is often helpful to ask a partner or relative to monitor Internet use. Reviewing one's own medical records is also prohibited.

Patients are not to ask for reassurance about health matters from friends and family members, and are not to discuss symptoms with others (e.g., "I have had this headache for two days now").

We suggest helping the patient draft a letter to friends and relatives explaining the detrimental effects of reassurance-seeking and providing suggestions for how to respond if asked for reassurance. For example, "I'm sorry but I can't answer your question because I agreed to help you with treatment."

Mental Analyzing. Patients are not to mentally devote time to going over what doctors have told them, or trying to analyze situations related to their health. Instead, they should purposely imagine being uncertain (as in exposure).

Clinical Pearl
Enlisting a Designated Support Person

Consider whether a partner or spouse or relative might be included in therapy

Some patients encounter difficulty conducting exposure and response prevention tasks independently between sessions. It may be useful in such cases to designate a "support person," such as a close friend or relative, who agrees to be available for the patient to assist with treatment when called upon by the patient. The support person should meet with the therapist to receive instruction on how to assist with treatment. The best support persons are those who are able to be empathetic yet firm. Individuals who are over-involved in the patient's symptoms, or who are overly critical or harsh, should be avoided. The support person should report any adherence problems to both the patient and therapist.

Clinical Pearl
Helping Patients Confront the Most Distressing Stimuli

For many patients, success with easier exercises predicts success with more challenging and anxiety-provoking tasks. However, if the going gets rough, convey sensitivity and understanding that such exercises are highly distressing. Also reiterate that this *temporary* distress is a necessary part of therapy. You can use the following tactics to help patients who are having difficulty attempting the most difficult exposures:

- Model the task prior to instructing the patient to engage.
- Use intermediate exposures that are of greater difficulty than those already conducted, but not as difficult as the planned task. The patient must agree that the intermediate step serves to facilitate eventual exposure with the more difficult item.
- DO NOT offer reassurance to the patient. Instead, use cognitive therapy techniques to identify and modify dysfunctional beliefs that are evoking high anxiety.
- Review evidence collected during previous exposures.
- Discuss the importance of learning to take acceptable risks.
- Revisit the importance of learning to tolerate uncertainty.

Dietary Restrictions. Patients are discouraged from taking dietary supplements, herbs, and other similar agents if their use reduces health anxiety or unexplained body sensations. Similarly, adhering to special diets *because of health anxiety* is prohibited.

The therapist should be alert for additional safety behaviors and signals that will require response prevention rules.

Homework Practice

Homework practice – a necessary part of the effectiveness of CBT

At the completion of each exposure session, assign homework practices for each day between sessions. Homework includes exposure, response prevention, and continual self-monitoring of health worries and any violations of response prevention rules. Consider the following points when designing homework assignments:

- Assign repetitions or variations of the in-session situational and interoceptive exposure exercises.
- Provide copies of the Exposure Practice Form (Appendix 11) to be completed during each homework assignment. Specify the details of each assignment on the form.
- Suggest that the patient review The 10 Tips for Exposure handout (Appendix 10) before each exposure exercise.
- Reinforce the importance of homework by beginning each session with a check of the previously assigned work.

Programmed and Lifestyle Exposure: Encouraging Independence

In this chapter, we primarily illustrate **programmed** exposure, in which the patient implements planned exercises under your direction at specific times and in particular locations. Patients must also engage in **lifestyle** exposure, which means making choices between sessions to take advantage of day-to-day opportunities to practice confronting, rather than avoiding, fear-provoking external stimuli and bodily sensations. In other words, they must practice *choosing to be anxious*. Encourage the patient to view spontaneously arising body sensations and other triggers as occasions to practice treatment techniques and work on further reducing health anxiety symptoms.

You should routinely remind patients that every choice they make regarding whether to confront or avoid a trigger makes a difference. Each time they choose to confront such a situation or resist seeking reassurance, health anxiety symptoms are weakened. However, when a decision is made to avoid a potential lifestyle exposure situation, these symptoms are strengthened.

Stylistic Considerations

Remarks During Exposure Tasks. Offering observations, praise, encouragement, and support during exposure maintains a strong therapeutic relationship. Ask the patient to tell you what he or she is learning through doing exposures. When exercises are proceeding as planned (i.e., anxiety levels are decreasing), the following sorts of comments and open-ended questions are helpful:

> **Conducting effective CBT is both a science and an art**

- "You're doing great. Remember, if you remain exposed to a situation, your anxiety level decreases on its own."
- "It looks like you're much less anxious now compared to when we started the session, and you haven't even attempted to seek any reassurance. How do you explain that your anxiety is lower?"
- "This seems like it's getting easier for you. You're weakening the link between this situation/sensation and anxiety. Good for you."
- "You see, as I told you before, you don't need to check or get reassurance to reduce your anxiety."

If the patient is having difficulty with anxiety during the exposure, convey that you understand how difficult this can be, but do not try to offer reassurance that medical symptoms are benign. Rather, remind the patient that with time and persistence, the exercises will become more manageable. Offer the following remarks:

- "Sometimes it takes a while for anxiety to go down. That means that you have to stick with the exposure even though it may be difficult. Eventually, you will begin to feel less distressed and you'll be glad you stuck with it."
- "This time your anxiety did not decrease by much, but we will keep working at it until it gets easier."

Dealing with Strong Urges to Ritualize. As individuals begin response prevention, they may have difficulty with strong urges to check, seek reassurance and perform other safety-related behaviors. Reviewing how such urges are learned responses to health-related thoughts and triggers, and how they diminish over time even if resisted, is useful in helping the patient resist violating response prevention instructions. The use of imagery can also be helpful, as in the example below.

> T: Is there something you could imagine, it doesn't matter what the image is, that will grab you and help you resist the urge to go the computer and look up explanations for symptoms? Perhaps you could imagine spraying the urge with a fire extinguisher, or surfing on the urge like a wave until it crests and breaks.

P: *(Smiling)* I know what I can imagine – I could picture you standing in front of the computer, waving your finger and shaking your head at me.

T: That's great. Should I look mean?

P: No, just having you there will help me.

T: That sounds like a good plan.

The therapist then had the patient practice using imagery in an imagined urge situation. This patient, who did not have access to a support person during treatment, found the imagery technique quite beneficial.

Humor. The use of humor or laughter to lighten the mood during therapy may be appropriate and can be beneficial, although it is not advisable in times of extreme distress. Follow the patient's lead and ensure that remarks remain relevant to the therapy discussion or exposure task, and do not distract the patient from the task.

4.1.6   Implementing Appropriate Self-Care Behaviors

Reviewing normal and healthy self-care behaviors

We find that despite their excessive health anxiety-related behaviors, most patients are actually aware of the appropriate ways to prevent or detect possible medical conditions. Thus, there is little risk of CBT resulting in the patient becoming indifferent to actual medical risks, giving up healthy illness screening and prevention behaviors, or waiting until it is too late to get help for a potentially life-threatening disease. Still, before ending treatment, it is appropriate to make sure the patient is aware of the appropriate and adaptive behaviors for prevention or early detection of medical conditions; especially those for which he or she might objectively be at elevated risk. For patients who are unaware of the proper self-care strategies, this might involve reviewing "fact sheets" from expert sources (e.g., the American Cancer Society) on how to screen for and detect illnesses (e.g., skin cancer), or attending a brief consultation with a medical professional to learn about the actual risks and prevention strategies.

4.2   Mechanisms of Action

How does exposure therapy work?

From a behavioral perspective, exposure techniques provide opportunities for the extinction of conditioned fear responses. Specifically, repeated and prolonged confrontation with feared stimuli produces decreases in conditioned fear (*habituation*). Response prevention aids this process by blocking the performance of behaviors which terminate anxiety before habituation can occur. From a cognitive perspective, CBT corrects dysfunctional beliefs that underlie health anxiety (e.g., misinterpretations of innocuous bodily sensations; exaggerated beliefs about illness risk) by presenting the patient with information that disconfirms these beliefs. Cognitive and psychoeducational interventions aim to modify these cognitions via a verbal-linguistic route, whereas exposure and response prevention accomplish the same goal experientially.

4.3 Efficacy and Prognosis

Randomized controlled studies indicate that CBT can produce clinically significant and lasting improvements in health anxiety symptoms (e.g., Clark et al., 1998; Greeven et al., 2007; Visser & Bouman, 2001; Warwick et al., 1996). Warwick and colleagues (1996) found significant reductions in reassurance-seeking, overall health anxiety, and checking frequency. General anxiety was reduced by approximately 70%, and depressive symptoms, by 53%. Moreover, CBT was accepted by patients: Only 6% of those recruited into the study refused to begin therapy, and another 6% dropped out of treatment prematurely. These findings suggest the specific procedures used in CBT for health anxiety, as opposed to non-specific factors (e.g., attention from the therapist), are the active ingredients for improvement, and are acceptable and tolerable for patients. Greeven and colleagues (2007) found that CBT was as effective as treatment with the antidepressant paroxetine.

Research demonstrates that the CBT approach outlined in this book can be very effective

A number of studies have examined the effectiveness of CBT within community clinics and hospitals (e.g., Bouton, 2002). In one investigation, Bleichhardt, Timmer, and Rief (2005) examined the effectiveness of CBT for two groups of health anxious individuals in a behavioral medicine inpatient unit: those with somatization disorder alone and those with somatization disorder and co-occurring hypochondriasis. The mean duration of treatment was 51.1 days and patients received individual CBT along with group problem-focused therapy, assertiveness training, and in some cases, treatment for other problems such as depression. Patients showed substantial long-term (1 year) reductions in intolerance of bodily complaints, general psychopathology, and the frequency of medical consultation. In addition, life satisfaction increased.

4.4 Variants of the Treatment Procedures

Visser and Bouman (2001) compared 12 weeks of CBT to 12 weeks of exposure therapy alone to a 12 week waiting-list control condition. Patients who received either active treatment showed significant improvement on all measures of health anxiety, general psychopathology, mood, and dysfunctional cognitions. No improvement was observed in the waiting-list condition. Immediately following treatment there were no differences in efficacy between CBT and exposure. At 7 months follow-up, the patients who had been treated remained improved without significant differences between active treatments. The most likely explanation for the comparable efficacy of CBT and exposure is that these treatments each incorporate elements of the other. That is, effective implementation of exposure requires the modification of dysfunctional beliefs. On the other hand, the CBT used in this study involved exposure-like techniques in the form of behavioral experiments, as described earlier in this chapter.

4.5 Problems in Carrying Out Treatment

4.5.1 Nonadherence

Once the patient understands and accepts the biopsychosocial model of health anxiety, the most common obstacle encountered in CBT is the patient's failure to follow through with treatment instructions. Many adherence problems can be prevented by clarifying how exposure and response prevention reduce excessive health concerns. In addition, the patient should be actively involved in the treatment planning process, and motivational interviewing techniques often will enhance adherence.

Noncompliance with Exposure

If a patient refuses to complete exposure tasks (e.g., homework assignments), ask him or her to explain this. Sometimes the problem can be addressed with simple problem-solving (e.g., time management). Also, make sure the exposure task itself is a good match to the patient's health-related worries. If not, the patient might perceive the exercise as irrelevant. If high levels of anxiety prompt refusal or "shortcuts" (e.g., subtle avoidance) during exposure, review the treatment rationale and use cognitive strategies to identify and address dysfunctional cognitions that underlie reluctance to confront the feared stimulus.

Refining the exposure hierarchy and adding intermediate items might be appropriate if the patient threatens to discontinue treatment. However, postponing exposures can reinforce avoidance. Thus, use this tactic only as a last resort. Instead, use Socratic questioning to create and amplify the discrepancy between non-adherence and the patient's goals. When nonadherence is perceived as conflicting with important personal goals (such as self-image, happiness, success), it increases motivation for change.

Noncompliance with Response Prevention

If the patient is deliberately concealing checking or reassurance-seeking behavior, explain the implications of this problem for treatment outcome in the following way:

T: Your wife called to tell me that you called your doctor several times last week when you felt tired or weak. She felt I needed to be aware of this because she was concerned that you weren't following the instructions we all agreed to at the beginning of therapy. We all agreed that if problems come up, you were going to get help from your wife instead of seeking reassurance. What happened?

If the patient makes a renewed agreement to adhere to the treatment instructions, the issue can be dropped. However, if repeated infractions occur, it may call for taking the time to remind the patient of the rationale for response prevention and to identify the possible practical barriers to adherence. The therapist and patient can also problem solve and examine cognitions that might interfere with adherence. As a last resort, it might be necessary to raise the possibility of suspending treatment. For example:

T: It seems that right now you aren't able to stop your reassurance-seeking as we agreed. If you cannot follow the treatment rules, we should talk about whether now is the right time for you to be doing this kind of therapy.

4.5.2 Arguments

Some patients become argumentative about the "strictness" of response prevention rules or the "dangerousness" of exposure tasks. You should resist the urge to lecture the patient, and instead use Socratic methods so that the belief-altering information is generated by the patient him or herself.

It is best to avoid rational debates and arguments over the patient's health or the riskiness of doing CBT

In the example below, the patient argues that speaking **one more time** with an infectious disease expert (Dr. B) would terminate his need for reassurance about Lyme disease:

P: I just <u>have</u> to ask Dr. B one more question about the symptoms of Lyme disease. I can't go on without asking.

T: I understand that you are anxious about this. Let's talk about that decision, though. You know that would be a violation of response prevention.

P: But I need to know. I think I might have some of the symptoms. You don't understand. I'm so worried.

T: What has Dr. B told you in the past when you've asked her about these kinds of symptoms?

P: That I'm fine. But this time it's different. I <u>really</u> feel like I could have Lyme disease. Please, just one more time. I have to ask her.

T: Oh, so, each time you've felt what you think are symptoms of Lyme disease, Dr. B. tells you that you are healthy. That's interesting. What do you think she'll say to you this time?

Clinical Pearl
When the Patient Argues

When a patient becomes argumentative (e.g., during exposure), it might indicate a rising level of distress. Instead of engaging in arguments about risk or the meaning of symptoms, the best strategy is to use conflict resolution strategies, such as the "broken record technique" (refrain from escalating the argument by restating your original point) or "turning the tables" (identify the problem and ask the patient what *he or she would do* to resolve it). Of course, set your limits and know how far it is reasonable to bend the therapy instructions. Statements such as the following might also be helpful:

- You are in treatment for yourself, not for me. So, I won't argue or debate with you. Engaging in treatment is entirely your choice. You stand to get better by trying these exercises and enduring the short-term anxiety. But you are also the one who has to live with the health anxiety if you choose not to do the therapy.
- Remember, we both agreed on the treatment plan. I expect you to hold up your end of the bargain.
- I agree with you that there is *some* risk involved, but it is not *high* risk. The goal of treatment is to weaken your anxiety about normal, but perhaps inexplicable body sensations.
- I know this is a difficult decision for you. Yet, if you are going to get over health anxiety, you have to confront your uncertainty and find out that the risk is low.

P: I hadn't thought about it that way before. You're right. She'll probably tell me the same thing.

T: OK, so if you already know what she'll say, would you agree that it would be more helpful for you to learn new ways of reducing your anxiety rather than asking Dr. B. for reassurances whenever you start worrying? We've discussed how the reassurance-seeking only makes your health concerns worse.

P: Yes. I see what you mean.

4.5.3   Unbearable Anxiety Levels During Exposure

If the patient becomes extremely anxious or emotional during an exposure, the task might be too difficult. In such cases, the exercise should be stopped and you should assess the underlying cognitions. If the patient is concerned that therapy is not working because anxiety fails to subside, emphasize that treatment requires continued practice. Point out that the patient took an important step simply by choosing to enter the feared situation in the first place.

4.6   Multicultural Issues

Numerous cultural factors can influence the assessment and treatment of health anxiety and it is best for the clinician to be aware of what these are

Cultural factors can influence the perception of bodily sensations, reflecting variability in cultural views of the relationship between body and mind. In Western cultures, for example, the predominant view is the *psychosomatic* perspective in which psychological distress is expressed as physical complaints. In many other cultures, however, the dominant view is the *somatopsychic* perspective in which physical problems are thought to produce emotional symptoms. Cultural differences also exist in the propensity to seek medical attention. Compared to other groups, for example, Asian American, African American, and Latino groups living in the United States show a stronger tendency to report medically unexplained symptoms to their physicians. Not surprisingly, the rates of diagnosis of health anxiety problems vary systematically by culture. Although there is no cross-cultural research addressing the treatment of health anxiety using CBT, it is important to attend to contextual factors when working with health anxious individuals from diverse ethnic and cultural backgrounds.

5

Case Vignette

This chapter presents a case example of health anxiety with a case formulation, fear hierarchy, and treatment plan.

Julia's Story

Julia, a 28-year old attorney, had always loved the outdoors. As a result of years of exposure to the sun, however, she had acquired countless freckles on her face, arms and legs; which she largely ignored. One day, she noticed a dime-shaped light brown discoloration near her hairline on her forehead. At her yearly medical exam, Julia asked her physician, Dr. Watson, to evaluate it for possible skin cancer. The doctor assessed her history, examined the discoloration closely, and even measured its diameter. Julia was informed that it was most likely a solar lentigo, a benign discoloration of the skin caused by sun exposure. Dr. Watson suggested she continue to wear sunscreen with zinc oxide to help prevent additional sun damage. There was no medical need at that time to biopsy or remove the lentigo, but Dr. Watson took a photograph of the lentigo in order to monitor its growth and coloration. He provided her with a copy of the photograph for her records. Julia felt relieved by this diagnosis and did not feel the need to have a dermatologist evaluate the discoloration given her doctor's confidence that it was benign.

Several years later, Julia's mother expressed concern that Julia's lentigo could be cancerous and suggested that she have it re-evaluated because other people in Julia's family had developed skin cancer in their 20s and 30s. Julia examined the spot in the mirror and looked at the photograph Dr. Watson had taken. Although there didn't seem to be any worsening, Julia became preoccupied with checking the lentigo every day for signs of skin cancer. She rubbed and picked at it to see if it was raised. She carried a mirror in her purse so she could check it any time of the day. After a week, Julia began thinking the previously diagnosed benign lentigo might have developed into cancer. It seemed larger, darker, and redder than before. She had the sensation that it was itchy and sore. She found herself noticing more freckles and other discolorations on her body, and she began checking them daily.

Julia began thinking about all the sun exposure she had over the years due to her love of the outdoors and having lived in sunny climates. She was now convinced that these behaviors, which she viewed as careless, had caused her "sun spots" and consequent skin cancer. She worried that she would die a slow and painful death from skin cancer.

Unable to tolerate her anxiety about the skin discoloration, and convinced that it was cancerous, Julia met with Dr. Watson. He evaluated the spot and compared it to her previous photograph, but again concluded that it was benign. Julia, however, was convinced that it was cancerous, and requested a referral to a dermatologist. Dr. Watson obliged and arranged an appointment with Dr. Haffer, a local dermatologist, who provided the same diagnosis and suggested that no follow-up was necessary. Dr. Haffer agreed that the area looked red and irritated, but she suggested this was due to Julia's frequent rubbing and picking. The dermatologist advised her to wear sunscreen with zinc oxide and a hat whenever exposed to the sun.

Julia continued to press Dr. Haffer for further work-up, with the physician stating the only way to 100% guarantee that the spot was in fact benign was to do an excision and biopsy. Dr. Haffer, however, did not advise this because she was convinced it was benign, and because the excision would leave a large scar on Julia's forehead.

Julia left the appointment initially relieved by the news that she did not have cancer, but later she became anxious when thinking about the fact that Dr. Haffer indicated the only way to confirm the benign nature of the discoloration was to do an involved and seemingly unnecessary excision. Suspecting that the spot was malignant, Julia began an exhaustive internet search on skin cancer. Every day, she examined images of benign and malignant discolorations and growths. She spoke with her family and friends about their knowledge of skin cancer. She frequently asked for reassurance that the "sun spot" was benign, never believing the feedback she received. She saw two more dermatologists, one affiliated with a large university hospital hours away from her home. Their diagnoses were consistent with the original one: benign solar lentigo. Julia began to avoid the sun altogether, eliminating many of her outdoor activities for fear of getting additional "sun spots." She used excessive amounts of sunscreen and wore large-brimmed hats to reduce sun exposure – even after dusk for fear that *any* remaining ultraviolet light could cause cancerous growths. At night, she would ruminate about the probability she had skin cancer, getting only 4 to 5 hours of sleep per night. Due to her numerous doctors' appointments and extensive internet searches, Julia's work performance was deteriorating.

Julia's mother noticed these changes in Julia and encouraged her to talk with a mental health professional. She asked Dr. Watson for a referral, and he connected her with a psychologist specializing in CBT for health anxiety.

Case Formulation

Julia's therapist used the biopsychosocial framework to generate a formulation of Julia's health anxiety symptoms and to derive a specific treatment plan. Julia had numerous benign skin discolorations due to years of outdoor activities. Due to her excessive checking, picking, and rubbing, the spot on her forehead had become irritated. Numerous triggers and cues to her health concerns were present in Julia's environment, including looking at herself in the mirror, seeing spots on her skin, and talking about cancer. Julia's belief that she had undiagnosed skin cancer led to anxiety, which maintained her excessive health concerns by causing her to feel stressed and fatigued. She had also become hypervigilant, checking endlessly for signs, sensations, and variations that only seemed to confirm her fears.

Julia's safety behaviors were conceptualized as natural responses to anxiety aimed at reducing distress and leading to some degree of certainty about the nature of her symptoms. These behaviors often resulted in temporary or short-lived reductions in anxiety. However, they ultimately maintained her health anxiety for the following reasons:

1. Body-checking led Julia to become sensitive to any changes on her skin.
2. Picking and rubbing led to irritation of her spots, which seemed to confirm (to Julia) that they were cancerous.
3. Reassurance-seeking from doctors, friends, family, and the internet always left some degree of ambiguity about the actual nature of the symptoms, thus sustaining belief that she had been misdiagnosed.
4. Excessive avoidance of sunlight prevented Julia from disconfirming dysfunctional beliefs such as "*any* sun exposure will cause cancer," "the only way to avoid skin cancer is to completely avoid the sun."

Fear Hierarchy

Julia and her therapist collaboratively developed the fear hierarchy that appears in Table 13.

Table 13
Julia's Fear Hierarchy

Hierarchy Item	SUDS
Look at images of benign skin discoloration	35
Look at images of malignant skin discolorations	45
Look at images of patients with cancer	45
Read a story about someone having skin cancer and dying	60
Write and read a story about her having skin cancer	80
Sun exposure with some skin exposed (no sleeves, scarves)	90
Sun exposure without a hat	90
Sun exposure with minimal (appropriate) sunscreen	100

Response Prevention Plan

Julia's response prevention plan was as follows:
- No checking of any spots on the skin
- No rubbing or picking at spots on the skin
- No asking questions for reassurance about skin cancer

- No internet searches on skin cancer and lentigenes
- No excessive sunscreen: Apply it only once in the morning

Treatment Plan

Julia's therapist created a treatment plan by matching the formulation components to the appropriate treatment techniques. Sessions 1 and 2 focused on conducting a functional assessment of her symptoms and initial self-monitoring. Psychoeducation was used to teach Julia about the biopsychosocial model of health anxiety, specifically about the possible origins of medically unexplained body sensations, the effects of anxious thinking, and the maladaptive effects of safety behaviors.

Sessions 3 and 4 utilized cognitive therapy techniques to help Julia identify and challenge dysfunctional beliefs, attitudes, and interpretations of health, illness and body symptoms. Her cognitive distortions were identified as including all-or-nothing thinking, negative interpretations, fortune-telling, intolerance of uncertainty, disqualifying, and lofty standards. Julia and her therapist began challenging and replacing these thinking patters with more realistic cognitions based on the medical evidence and the psychoeducational modules.

Sessions 5–10 included exposure, response prevention, and challenging cognitive distortions. Situational, imaginal, and interoceptive exposures were planned and conducted gradually, beginning with moderately difficult tasks and working up to highly anxiety-inducing ones. Simultaneously, Julie practiced refraining from anxiety-reducing behaviors (i.e., response prevention). Exposure and response prevention practice taught Julia that anxiety is temporary and that safety behaviors are not necessary to reduce anxiety. She also began to believe more strongly that her avoidance and safety behaviors were not necessary to prevent cancer.

During sessions 11–14 Julia was encouraged to be her own therapist and to determine the next steps in treatment. This afforded her the opportunity to fine-tune her newly-acquired skills and to become independent in her practice of effectively managing her own health anxiety. Sessions 15 and 16 involved wrapping up and planning for the future; with the goal of Julia being able to maintain her treatment gains. Julie was very aware of the appropriate and adaptive ways to take care of her skin and when it might be important to seek medical attention. Given her elevated risk of skin cancer, she and her therapist developed a list of healthy self-care strategies (e.g., appropriate use of sun screen, times of the day to avoid lengthy exposure to direct sunlight); which Julie agreed to adhere to, but not take to extremes. Julie made excellent progress, with significant reductions in health anxiety and urges to use safety behaviors. Additionally, she became less preoccupied with her skin spots and was able to behave in ways consistent with good health.

6

Further Reading

1. Abramowitz, J., & Braddock, A. E. (2008). *Psychological treatment of health anxiety and hypochondriasis: A biopsychosocial approach.* Cambridge, MA: Hogrefe and Huber. Presents didactic material on the clinical features and psychological theories of health anxiety. Also contains a manual for cognitive-behavioral assessment and treatment.
2. Taylor, S., & Asmundson, G. (2004). *Treating health anxiety.* New York, NY: Guilford. This book provides the reader with an in-depth review of health anxiety symptoms and theories, emphasizing cognitive-behavioral theory. The use of behavioral and cognitive therapy techniques is also described in detail.
3. Furer, P., Walker, J. R., & Stein, M. B. (2007). *Treating health anxiety and fear of death: A practitioner's guide.* New York, NY: Springer. This book presents a description of health anxiety as well as the fear of death, and reviews the literature on the nature and treatment of these conditions. Cognitive-behavioral therapy for these problems is also described in detail.

7

References

Abramowitz, J. S., & Braddock, A. E. (2008). *Psychological treatment of health anxiety and hypochondriasis: A biopsychosocial approach*. Cambridge, MA : Hogrefe & Huber.

American Psychiatric Association (1994). *Diagnostic and Statistical Manual of Mental Disorders* (4th ed.). Washington, DC: Author.

American Psychiatric Association (2000). *Diagnostic and Statistical Manual of Mental Disorders* (4th edition, text revision). Washington, DC: Author.

Amrhein, P. C., Miller, W. R., Yahne, C. E., Palmer, M., & Fulcher, L. (2003). Client commitment language during Motivational Interviewing predicts drug use outcomes. *Journal of Consulting and Clinical Psychology, 71*, 862–878.

Barlow, D. H., Craske, M., Cerny, J., & Klosko, J. (1989). Behavioral treatment of panic disorder. *Behavior Therapy, 30*, 261–282.

Barsky, A. J., Cleary, P. D., Wyshak, G., Spitzer, R. L., Williams, J. B. W., & Klerman, G. L. (1992). A structured diagnostic interview for hypochondriasis: A proposed criterion standard. *Journal of Nervous and Mental Disease, 180*, 20-27.

Beck, A.T. (1976). *Cognitive therapy and the emotional disorders*. New York, NY: International University Press.

Beck, A. T., Steer, R. A., & Brown, G. K. (1996). *Manual for Beck Depression Inventory-II*. San Antonio, TX: Psychological Corporation.

Bleichhardt, G., Timmer, B., & Rief, W. (2005). Hypochondriasis among patients with multiple somatoform symptoms: Psychopathology and outcome of a cognitive- behavioral therapy. *Journal of Contemporary Psychotherapy, 35(3)*, 239–249.

Bouton, M. E. (2002). Context, ambiguity, and unlearning: Sources of relapse after behavioral extinction. *Biological Psychiatry, 52*, 976–986.

Brown, T. A., DiNardo, P., & Barlow, D. H. (1994). *Anxiety disorders interview schedule for DSM-IV*. San Antonio, TX: The Psychological Corporation.

Clark, D. M., Salkovskis, P. M., Hackmann, A., Wells, A., Fennell, M., Ludgate, J., ... Gelder, M. (1998). Two psychological treatments for hypochondriasis: A randomized controlled trial. *British Journal of Psychiatry, 173*, 218–225.

Eisen, J. L., Phillips, K. A., Baer, L., Beer, D. A., Atala, K. D., & Rasmussen, S. A. (1998). The Brown Assessment of Beliefs Scale: reliability and validity. *American Journal of Psychiatry, 155*, 102–108.

Fallon, B. A., Javitch, J. A., Hollander, E., & Liebowitz, M. R. (1991). Hypochondriasis and obsessive-compulsive disorder: Overlaps in diagnosis and treatment. *Journal of Clinical Psychiatry, 52*, 457–460.

Fallon, B. A., Liebowitz, M. R., Salman, E., Schneier, F. R., Insino, C., Hollander, E., & Klein, D. F. (1993). Fluoxetine for hypochondriachal patients without major depression. *Journal of Clinical Psychopharmacology, 13*, 438–441.

Fallon, B. A., Schneier, F. R., Marchall, R., Campeas, R., Vermes, D., Goetz, D., & Liebowitz, M. R. (1996). The pharmacotherapy of hypochondriasis. *Psychopharmacology Bulletin, 32*, 607–611.

Fallon, B. A., Quershi, A. I., Schneier, F. R., Sanchez-Lacay, A., Vermes, D., Feinstein, R., ... Liebowitz, M. R. (2003). An open trial of fluvoxamine for hypochondriasis. *Psychosomatics, 44(4)*, 298–303.

Fallon, B. A. (1999). Somatoform disorders. In R.E. Feinstein & A.A. Brewer (Eds.), *Primary care psychiatry and behavioral medicine: Brief office treatment and management pathways* (pp. 146–170). New York, NY: Springer.

Fallon, B. A. (2001). Pharmacologic strategies for hypochondriasis. In V. Starcevic & D.R. Lipsitt (Eds.), *Hypochondriasis: Modern perspectives on an ancient malady* (pp. 329–351). New York, NY: Oxford University Press.

First, M. B., Spitzer, R. L., Gibbon, M., & Williams, J. B. W. (1996). *Structured Clinical Interview for DSM-IV Axis I Disorders-Patient Edition (SCID-I/P, Version 2.0)*. New York, NY: Biometrics Research Department, New York State Psychiatric Institute.

Goodman, W. K., Price, L. H., Rasmussen, S. A., Mazure, C., Delgado, P., Heninger, G. R., & Charney, D. S. (1989). The Yale-Brown Obsessive Compulsive Scale: validity. *Archives of General Psychiatry, 46*, 1012–1016.

Goodman, W. K., Price, L. H., Rasmussen, S. A., Mazure, C., Fleischmann, R. L., Hill, C. L., ... Charney, D. S. (1989). The Yale-Brown Obsessive Compulsive Scale: development, use, and reliability. *Archives of General Psychiatry, 46*, 1006–1011.

Greeven, A., van Balkom, A., Visser, S., Merkelbach, J., van Rood, Y., van Dyck, R., ... Spinhoven, P. (2007). Cognitive-behavior therapy and paroxetine in the treatment of hypochondriasis: a randomized controlled trial. *American Journal of Psychiatry, 164*, 91–99.

Hadjistavropoulos, H. D., Frombach, I. K., & Asmundson, G. J. G. (1999). Exploratory and confirmatory factor analytic investigations of the Illness Attitudes Scales in a nonclinical sample. *Behavior Research and Therapy, 37*, 671–684.

Kamlana, S. H, & Gray, P. (1988). Fear of AIDS. *British Journal of Psychiatry, 15*, 1291.

Kellner, R. (1986). *Somatization and hypochondriasis*. New York, NY: Praeger-Greenwood.

Kellner, R. (1987). *Abridged manual of the Illness Attitude Scales*. Unpublished manual, Department of Psychiatry, School of Medicine, University of New Mexico, Albuquerque.

Kjernisted, K. D., Enns, M. W., & Lander, M. (2002). An open-label clinical trial of nefazodone in hypochondriasis. *Psychosomatics, 43*, 290–294.

Lippert, G. P. (1986). Excessive concern about AIDS in two bisexual men. *Canadian Journal of Psychiatry, 31*, 63–65.

Lovibond, S. H., & Lovibond, P. F. (1995). *Manual for the Depression Anxiety Stress Scales* (2nd ed.). Sydney, Australia: Psychology Foundation.

Miller, W. R., & Rollnick, S. (2002). *Motivational interviewing: Preparing people for change* (2nd ed.). New York, NY: Guilford.

Oosterbaan, D.B., van Balkom, A.J.L.M., van Boeijen, C.A., de Meij, T.G.J., & van Dyck, R. (2001). An open study of paroxetine in hypochondriasis. *Progress in Neuro-Psychopharmacology and Biological Psychiatry, 25*, 1023–1033.

Rief, W., Hiller, W., & Margraf, J. (1998). Cognitive aspects of hypochondriasis and the somatization syndrome. *Journal of Abnormal Psychology, 107*, 587–595.

Spitzer, R., Kroenke, K., & Williams, J. (1999). Validation and utility of a self-report version of PRIME-MD: the PHQ primary care study. Primary care evaluation of mental disorders. Patient Health Questionnaire. *Journal of the American Medical Association, 282*, 1737–1744.

Salkovskis, P. M., Rimes, K. A., Warwick, H. M., & Clark, D. M. (2002). The Health Anxiety Inventory: Development and validation of scales for the measurement of health anxiety and hypochondriasis. *Psychological Medicine, 32*, 843–853.

Salkovskis, P., Warwick, H., & Deale, A. (2003). Cognitive-behavioral treatment for severe and persistent health anxiety (hypochondriasis). *Brief Treatment and Crisis Intervention, 3*, 353–367.

Sheehan, D., Lecrubier, Y., Harnett-Sheehan, K., Amoriam, P., Janavs, J., Weiller, E., ... Dunbar, G. (1998). The Mini International Neuropsychiatric Interview (M.I.N.I.) The development and validation of a structured diagnostic interview. *Journal of Clinical Psychiatry, 59*(Suppl. 20), 22–23.

Stone, A.B. (1993). Treatment of hypochondriasis with clomipramine. *Journal of Clinical Psychiatry, 54*, 200–201.

Visser, S. & Bouman, T. (2001). The treatment of hypochondriasis: Exposure plus response prevention versus cognitive therapy, *Behaviour Research and Therapy, 39*, 423–442.

Warwick, H. M., Clark, D. M., Cobb, A. M., & Salkovskis, P. M. (1996). A controlled trial of cognitive-behavioral treatment of hypochondriasis. *British Journal of Psychiatry, 169*, 189–195.

8

Appendices: Tools and Resources

The following tools and resources are found in the appendices:
Appendix 1: Functional Assessment Form
Appendix 2: Self-Monitoring of Body Symptoms Form
Appendix 3: Symptom Record
Appendix 4: Our Noisy Bodies
Appendix 5: The Fight-or-Flight Response
Appendix 6: Body Symptom Handout
Appendix 7: Common Thinking Patterns in Health Anxiety
Appendix 8: Helpful Comments
Appendix 9: Exposure Hierarchy Form
Appendix 10: 10 Tips for Successful Exposure
Appendix 11: Exposure Practice Form
Appendix 12: Help with Response Prevention

Functional Assessment Form

Patient's name: _____

Age _____

Duration of symptoms: _____

Educational level: _____

Occupation: _____

Relationship status: _____

Current living arrangement: _____

I. Triggers

A. Physical signs, sensations, perturbations (bodily signs and "symptoms" that evoke health concerns; e.g., headaches, bumps on the skin, lightheadedness)

B. External stimuli (e.g., hospitals, new stories about illnesses)

From: J. S. Abramowitz & A. E. Braddock: *Hypochondriasis and Health Anxiety*　　　© 2011 Hogrefe Publishing

II. Cognitive Features (Dysfunctional beliefs)

A. Misinterpretations of bodily signs and sensations (e.g., "when I have a headache, it means I have a brain tumor"; "When I notice a lump in my throat I think it means my airway is closing in")

B. Feared consequences of exposure to external cues (e.g., "If I read about cancer, I will think I have all the symptoms"; "If I go to a hospital, I will get sick")

C. Dysfunctional health-related beliefs (e.g., concerning general health/illness, vulnerability to sicknesses, beliefs about doctors and medicine, beliefs about death)

III. Behaviors

A. Passive avoidance and its relationship to health anxiety (e.g., avoids books and movies about illnesses to keep from thinking about illnesses; avoids doctors because of the fear of being told he/she is really sick)

B. Body monitoring and checking (describe in detail) and its relationship to health anxiety (e.g., checking color and odor of stool, excessive monitoring of vital signs, repetitive checking the body for lumps, etc.)

C. Reassurance-seeking and other forms of checking (e.g., looking up symptoms in books or on the Internet, excessive doctor visits for tests/exams/consults, discussing symptoms with others or asking excessive questions)

D. Safety signals (stimuli and behaviors associated with the absence of illness; e.g., sitting down when notices sensations, keeping bottle of water on hand)

From: J. S. Abramowitz & A. E. Braddock: *Hypochondriasis and Health Anxiety*   © 2011 Hogrefe Publishing

Self-Monitoring of Body Symptoms Form

Instructions: For one week, note each body symptom that occurs, the time it started and ended, its severity, and the situation in which it occurred. Record this information as soon as the sensation occurs so that this diary is accurate.

Symptom	Time (start/end)	Severity (0–10)	Situation

From: J. S. Abramowitz & A. E. Braddock: *Hypochondriasis and Health Anxiety*   © 2011 Hogrefe Publishing

Symptom Record

Date: _____ Time began: _____ AM/PM   Time ended_____ AM/PM

Trigger: What symptom(s) did you notice first? _____

_____

_____

Other Bodily Symptoms

❑ Trembling	❑ Muscle tension/ache	❑ Restlessness
❑ Fatigue	❑ Difficulty breathing	❑ Racing heart
❑ Sweating	❑ Dry mouth	❑ Dizzy/lightheaded
❑ Nausea/diarrhea	❑ Hot flashes/chills	❑ Frequent urination
❑ Trouble swallowing	❑ Keyed up/on edge	❑ Irritable
❑ Trouble sleeping	❑ Difficulty concentrating	❑ Jumpy/easily startled

How concerned were you? *(circle)*

0	1	2	3	4	5	6	7	8
None		Mild		Moderate		Strong		Extreme

What did the symptoms mean to you?: _____

_____

_____

What did you do?

❑ Check body	❑ Call doctor	❑ Check medical reference
❑ Visit doctor	❑ Just worry	❑ Check with friend/relative
❑ Distract yourself	❑ Analyze the situation	❑ Discuss the symptoms with someone else

Other actions: _____

From: J. S. Abramowitz & A. E. Braddock: *Hypochondriasis and Health Anxiety*   © 2011 Hogrefe Publishing

Our Noisy Bodies

What Is Body Noise and What Causes It?

The human body is in a constant state of flux. Whether we are awake or sleeping, there is always activity in our bodies – they are always changing. The purpose of this handout is to teach you about unwanted bodily sensations – or what we'll call *body noise* – and the various explanations for it. To help, you might think of the human body as similar to other complex machines such as computers and automobiles. These machines, even when working properly, often make strange noises such as clicking, whirring, buzzing, screeching, among other noises. As with such machinery, even a generally healthy human body produces all sorts of physical symptoms that might be painful, unexpected, and otherwise unwanted. Accordingly, the first aim of this handout is to help you understand that there are numerous explanations for the uncomfortable body sensations you experience.

Homeostasis

One of the most remarkable properties of the human body is *homeostasis*. Homeostasis refers to the process by which the body reacts to changes in the environment in order to maintain its internal balances. The body's reactions include countless dynamic and interconnected mechanisms, some of which might not be noticeable to the person, and others of which – such as feelings of nausea, pain, rapid heartbeat, hot and cold feelings, and fatigue – might be quite noticeable.

The control of body temperature in humans is a good example of how homeostasis works. In human beings normal body temperature fluctuates around the value of 98.6°F, but various factors can raise or lower body temperature including exposure to certain environmental conditions (e.g., extreme cold), hormone levels, metabolic rate, and even infections. The body's temperature regulation is controlled by a region in the brain called the hypothalamus. Feedback about body temperature is carried through the bloodstream to the brain and it results in adjustments in breathing and heart rate, and blood sugar levels. For instance, when the body becomes overheated, blood sugar levels decline causing us to feel fatigued so that we reduce our activity to cool off. We also perspire, which leads to evaporation and cooling of the skin. Because many of these changes are abrupt and uncomfortable, they can be misinterpreted as signs of a medical condition.

It is impossible to list all of the bodily signs and symptoms associated with homeostasis in this handout (entire books have been written on the subject), and everyone's body functions a little differently. However, when physical symptoms are experienced in the absence of laboratory or diagnostic evidence of a medical illness, a likely explanation is that the unpleasant feelings are probably effects of one or more homeostatic functions.

Shifts in Your Daily Routine

Most of us follow a fairly consistent pattern of daily activities. We go to sleep and wake up at around the same time. We go through the same activities when getting prepared for the day and when unwinding before bedtime. We eat our meals around the same time each day. We even go to many of the same places (work, school) on a regular basis. As mentioned above, our bodies are very good at adjusting to these routines. In fact, perhaps our bodies adjust *too* well, since it doesn't take much of a change in routine to produce noticeable physical effects, as is discussed below.

Our diet provides a nice illustration of just how sensitive our bodies are to changes in daily routine. The human body adapts to our eating schedule, the kinds of foods we eat, and the quantity of food we eat. So, if we skip a meal, the body's rhythm is thrown off which can produce feelings of tiredness, headaches, changes in blood pressure, heart rate, breathing rate, and changes in blood sugar levels, which can make one feel faint. When we try new foods, perhaps those high in fiber or with lots of

From: J. S. Abramowitz & A. E. Braddock: *Hypochondriasis and Health Anxiety* spices, it can take the stomach by surprise leading to gas, cramps, stomach aches, and changes in the color, smell, and consistency of urine and feces. Finally, eating a lot more (or less) food than we typically do can lead to similar symptoms.

Our muscles and joints also acclimate to our typical activity level and can become strained, which produces pain and tightness, if we are more active than usual or if we use our muscles for activities that we don't usually perform. For example, if you enjoy playing tennis or softball, yet only play once in a while (or it it's the first game after a long break), you will probably experience soreness or tightness in your arms and chest afterward. This is because your muscles are not used to swinging or throwing since you don't engage in these activities on a regular basis. The same thing happens if you suddenly do heavy lifting that you don't normally do. Many people harmlessly pull muscles in their arms or chest this way and then confuse the pain and tightness for a more serious problem, such as a heart attack.

Sometimes, whether planned or unplanned, we don't get as much sleep as we should, or as we are used to. This is another example of how the body can produce strange and uncomfortable symptoms that are not indications of a serious medical problem. When we don't get a good night's sleep, it is common to feel weak and lethargic, have trembles, lose our appetite, get a headache, and even experience dizziness, tingling, a racing heart, or have unusual visual experiences (flashes of light). Of course, it is very easy to interpret these signs and sensations as indicating a serious problem, but they are actually ways that our body tells us that we should get more sleep.

Minor Medical Conditions

Many minor ailments can produce very noticeable body changes. For example, even a cold, allergic reaction, or small infection can produce tenderness, soreness, swollen lymph nodes, racing heart, shortness of breath, and sneezing and coughing leading to a sore, dry, or scratchy throat. Allergens can also lead to hives, which are red itchy marks on the skin, or welts, which are similar to hives but occur under the skin. Heartburn and acid reflux can produce chest or stomach pain and burning in the throat. Irritable bowel syndrome (IBS) is a benign, yet uncomfortable condition characterized by abdominal pain, bowel cramps and urgency, diarrhea, bloating, constipation, and gas. It is exacerbated by eating certain foods such as tomatoes, spices, red meat, and fatty foods. Although the discomfort associated with IBS is benign, people often misinterpret these symptoms, and also those of hemorrhoids (which can produce pain and bloody stools), for more serious medical problems. Another benign, yet frightening, condition is called "unexplained cutaneous sensory syndrome," which can include skin pain, rash, numbness, and itching. Finally, hyperhidrosis is a harmless condition (yet sometimes embarrassing) in which the person perspires excessively from the hands, face, and other parts of the body.

Orthostatic Intolerance

Orthostatic intolerance refers to how well the body makes the necessary adjustments to counteract gravity. That is, when we stand up from a seated or prone (laying down) position, our circulatory system needs to work a little harder so that gravity does not pull all of our blood down to our legs and feet. As we age, most everyone experiences normal episodes of orthostatic hypotension in which blood pressure drops as a result of simply moving to a standing position. This might be especially noticeable when getting out of bed first thing in the morning, and can involve a number of uncomfortable sensations such as a noticeable increase in heart rate, feelings of nausea, vertigo, lightheadedness and faintness (although actually fainting is rare), headaches, and fatigue.

Health Habits

Certain habits, some of which might be very subtle, can also result in uncomfortable body symptoms. For instance, eating and drinking rapidly, chewing gum, and smoking, can cause aerophagia (literally

From: J. S. Abramowitz & A. E. Braddock: *Hypochondriasis and Health Anxiety*   © 2011 Hogrefe Publishing

meaning "swallowing air"), a benign condition that produces discomfort and bloating in the stomach, and sometimes chronic belching. Breathing heavily can result in feelings of faintness, tingling in the extremities, racing heart, and sweating since the muscles of the chest are working overtime to inhale and exhale.

Mind-Body Connection

It is easy to overlook the mind-body connection as a factor in the production of body symptoms. But, all of our emotional reactions (sadness, fear, anxiety, anger, and even excitement and elation) have a physical component. Specifically, emotions are accompanied by activation of the body's sympathetic nervous system and the release of adrenaline (also known as epinephrine). This activity produces a set of perceptible and sometimes intense body changes including (but not limited to) increased heart rate and strength of heart beat, increased speed and depth of breathing, increased muscle tension, dilation of the pupils which can produce strange visual experiences (spots or flashes of light), perspiration, dry mouth, decreased activity in the digestive system, and increased urges to use the bathroom. Some emotions, such as disgust, are associated with a reduction in blood pressure and heart rate, and a reduction in muscle tension.

Although they can seem intense and uncomfortable, these body sensations are harmless. In fact, these reactions are part of the body's natural "fight-or-flight" response. Even prolonged activation of the fight-or-flight response is not dangerous, although this, too, can produce additional frightening body symptoms such as exhaustion and fatigue from the increase in activity within the body, faintness and feelings of unreality from hyperventilation and the body's conversion of oxygen to carbon dioxide, blurred vision and spots from pupil dilation, numbness and tingling in the extremities from blood vessel constriction, breathlessness and feelings of choking or smothering from the increased rate and depth of breathing, aches, pains, tightness, trembling, and twitching from muscle tension, hot or cold flashes from sweating, and nausea and constipation from reduced digestive system activity.

Attention and Body Focus

Any discussion of body symptoms would be incomplete without also covering the importance of paying attention to these symptoms. Attention strongly influences how we experience body symptoms since the more we think about a symptom, the more the symptom will bother us. Therefore, the second aim of this handout is to help you understand how paying close attention to body symptoms actually makes them become more intense.

What Determines Body Focus?

As this handout describes, everyone experiences constant noise in their body (with all of this noise, it's a wonder we can ever pay attention to anything else!). However, some people focus very much on their body, whereas others tend not to. There are three reasons for this. First, some people are simply more focused and attentive than others – perhaps because of their personality. So, in addition to being focused on external events, such people are also tuned in to internal bodily events.

Second, the degree to which someone is body-focused can be influenced by how much the people around them are talking about and calling attention to body symptoms. For example, if someone is repeatedly asked, "How is your _____ doing today," this will keep them focused on the particular symptom. Similarly, when the media popularizes illnesses, such as West Nile virus or Lyme disease, it causes people to attend more closely to body sensations.

Finally, focusing on symptoms is influenced by the degree to which the person is concerned with some aspect of their health. Research demonstrates that people who think they might have a medical problem tend to focus and concentrate on (even to the point of "looking for") body symptoms that they

From: J. S. Abramowitz & A. E. Braddock: *Hypochondriasis and Health Anxiety*   © 2011 Hogrefe Publishing

think *could be* a sign of the medical problem. This leads them to notice more symptoms, become more concerned, and so on. The result is a vicious cycle that can be hard to stop by yourself.

How Body Focus and Attention Increase Body Noise

Research consistently shows that when we focus attention on something, we tend to notice it more. In one study, for example, healthy participants who were instructed to deliberately focus on their bodies reported more symptoms than those given instructions to focus elsewhere. In fact, those people who focused on their bodies reported more painful and bothersome body symptoms. So, focusing on a particular symptom will give the symptom a "life of its own." The symptom becomes more threatening and disturbing. This makes us focus even more intently on the details and subtleties of the symptoms, making it seem as if we are developing more intense symptoms, which we might interpret as a sign that things are getting worse. Of course, at this point, we don't stop to consider that what we assume are serious medical symptoms might be body noise resulting from a benign cause.

Summary

To summarize the main points of this handout, body symptoms have real physical causes. However, not all body symptoms are caused by serious medical problems. Symptoms are often the result of the body's tendency to maintain a relatively constant internal state (homeostasis) and can result from changes in daily routine, activity levels, diet, certain health habits, minor ailments, emotional reactions, among other factors. Moreover, how much attention we give to body sensations influences the way we experience these sensations. People who, for whatever reason, are closely tuned in to their bodies, will notice more sensations and experience them as more intense. When this occurs, the chances increase that these benign body symptoms will be incorrectly interpreted as signs of a more serious medical condition.

From: J. S. Abramowitz & A. E. Braddock: *Hypochondriasis and Health Anxiety*   © 2011 Hogrefe Publishing

The Fight-or-Flight Response

What Is the Fight-or-Flight Response?

When a person perceives that danger is possible, such as when he or she interprets a situation or stimulus in a threatening way, there is an automatic physiological (bodily) response that takes over and helps protect the person from danger. This is called the "**fight-or-flight response**" because its purpose is to help you either fight or flee from potential danger. When our ancestors lived among other animals out in the wilds, it was important for their survival that when faced with danger, an automatic "alarm" response would take over causing them to take immediate action (attack or run). The fight-or-flight response is still an important mechanism, even in today's world. Think of what would happen if a bus was speeding toward you, horn blasting, and you experienced no sense of danger or alarm. You would probably be killed. Luckily, your fight-or-flight response automatically steps in and takes over, making you get safely out of the way. Again, the purpose of this response is to protect you and keep you alive.

When a person perceives danger, his or her brain sends messages to a part the nervous system called the autonomic nervous system. The autonomic nervous system has two subsections or branches called the **sympathetic nervous system** and the **parasympathetic nervous system**. It is these two branches of the nervous system which are directly involved in controlling the body's energy levels and preparation for action. Very simply, the sympathetic nervous system is the fight-or-flight system which gets the body aroused and ready for action (fighting or fleeing), and the parasympathetic nervous system returns the body to a normal, non-aroused state.

When activated, the sympathetic nervous system releases a chemical called **adrenalin**. Adrenalin is used as a messenger to continue sympathetic nervous system activity, so that once activity begins, it often continues and increases for some time. However, sympathetic nervous system activity is stopped in two ways. First, the adrenalin is eventually destroyed by other chemicals in the body. Second, eventually, the body "has enough" of the fight-or-flight response and activates the parasympathetic nervous system to restore a relaxed feeling. In other words, the response does not continue forever, nor does it spiral out of control or intensify to "damaging levels." First, the fight-or-flight response is not at all dangerous – it is meant to help you, not harm you. Second, the parasympathetic nervous system is an inbuilt protector which slows down the sympathetic nervous system after a while.

Another important point is that adrenalin takes time to fully exit the blood stream. So, even after your sympathetic nervous system has stopped responding, you are likely to feel keyed up or alarmed for some time because the adrenalin is still floating around in your system. This is actually part of the protective mechanism since in the wild, danger often has a habit of returning. So, it is useful for us to remain in fight-or-flight mode so that we can quickly react if danger returns.

Bodily Symptoms Associated with the Fight-or-Flight Response

The fight-or-flight response is associated with changes in the body that can be intense, and that can mimic medical problems. It is therefore important for you to understand what these bodily symptoms and sensations are, and what purposes they serve. Keep in mind that the overall purpose of the fight-or-flight response is to protect you from danger. Its physical symptoms, therefore, are all intended to prepare you to fight or flee. We will next review each type of body symptom.

From: J. S. Abramowitz & A. E. Braddock: *Hypochondriasis and Health Anxiety*   © 2011 Hogrefe Publishing

Breathing Symptoms

During the fight-or-flight response your breathing automatically becomes faster and deeper. This occurs in order to increase the amount of oxygen you take in since the body needs higher levels of oxygen to be able to fight or flee. Oxygen is used by the muscles to make energy for fighting or fleeing danger.

The high rate and depth of breathing sometimes causes harmless but unpleasant symptoms such as breathlessness, feelings of choking or smothering, and pains or tightness in the chest. Also, blood supply to the head may be temporarily decreased. While this is only a small amount and is not at all dangerous, it produces unpleasant (but harmless) symptoms including dizziness, lightheadedness, blurred vision, confusion, feeling of unreality (or, feeling as if you are in a dream state), and hot flushes.

Heart and Cardiovascular Symptoms

In order to efficiently circulate oxygen and nutrients to your muscles for fighting or fleeing, your heart rate and the strength of your heartbeat both increase during fight or flight. There is also a change in blood flow patterns so that blood is taken away from places where it is not needed (by a tightening of the blood vessels) and toward places where it is needed more (by dilation of the blood vessels). For example, blood is taken away from the skin, fingers, and toes. This is useful because having less blood flow to these areas means we are less likely to bleed to death if we are cut while fighting or fleeing. As a result of this reaction, however, your skin might turn pale or feel cold, especially your hands and feet. The blood instead goes to large muscles, such as the thighs, heart, and biceps, which need the oxygen for fighting or fleeing.

Other Symptoms

The fight-flight response also increases sweating. Sweat (perspiration) is the body's inbuilt air conditioning system. When sweat evaporates, it cools the body to prevent it from overheating, and thus allows us to continue fighting or fleeing from danger without becoming exhausted from heat.

Your pupils also become dilated (widened) to let in more light during fight or flight. This helps people scan the surroundings for danger. It also helps us see better in the dark. However, there may be temporary unpleasant side effects of pupil dilation, such as blurred vision, spots in front of the eyes, or being overly sensitivity to light.

During fight-or-flight, activity in the digestive system also decreases. After all, digesting food is not as important as fighting off danger or fleeing to safety. The energy needed to digest food is therefore used for more immediate survival purposes. A side effect of decreased digestive system activity is a decrease in salivation, which leads to dry or "cotton" mouth. Another side effect is nausea, heavy feelings in the stomach, and sometimes diarrhea.

Muscle groups tense up in preparation for fight or flight, and this causes feelings of tension. This tension may occur in the form of trembling or shaking, as well as other medically unexplained symptoms such as body movements, twitching, or eye blinking. It is also common to experience aches and pains (e.g., joint pain, headaches) associated with prolonged fight or flight, and this is a direct result of extended periods of muscle tension.

The fight-or-flight response involves activation and arousal of many of the body's systems and large muscle groups. This takes a lot of energy, and therefore people often feel exhausted, drained, and washed out during and after experiencing this type of arousal.

Finally, the fight-or-flight response leads to an increase in alertness and attention. In particular, attention is focused on the source of the perceived threat or danger. This is a very useful effect of the fight-or-flight system because if we didn't pay attention to things that could harm us, we probably wouldn't survive. When it seems like we are preoccupied or unable to take our minds off of something threatening that has caught our attention, it is a natural consequence of this system.

From: J. S. Abramowitz & A. E. Braddock: *Hypochondriasis and Health Anxiety*   © 2011 Hogrefe Publishing

Common Misperceptions of Fight-or-Flight Symptoms

It is easy to misunderstand the symptoms associated with fight-or-flight as those of a serious medical problem. Shortness of breath, twitching, lightheadedness, diarrhea, among other symptoms *can* be signs of more serious conditions. Common mistaken ideas and interpretations of the fight-or-flight symptoms include beliefs about losing control, collapsing, cardiac problems, and neurological problems such as having a stroke or fainting. Let's look more closely at each of these conditions:

Losing Control
Some people, when they experience the fight-or-flight response, believe they are going to lose control, become paralyzed, or lose their judgment and begin acting in strange or terrible ways (e.g., hurting people, saying inappropriate things). Or, they may simply have the overwhelming feeling that something bad is going to happen.

From reading this handout, you now know where this feeling comes from: The fight-or-flight response involves the entire body becoming prepared for action, and there is a strong feeling like you need to escape. However, the fight-or-flight response is not aimed at hurting people who are not a threat, and it will not produce paralysis. Rather, the entire response is designed to get you away from potential danger. People do not "go crazy" or "lose control" when they experience fight-or-flight. Remember that the fight-or-flight system is designed to help you when you are in threatening situations. So, although it might seem like you are confused or disoriented, you are actually able to think faster and react more quickly (you are physically stronger and your reflexes are quicker) than you normally would. This is the same thing that happens when a person is in a real emergency. Think of people who accomplish amazing things (such as lifting extremely heavy objects) and overcome their own intense fears under dire circumstances in order to save themselves or their children.

Heart Conditions
It is easy to mistake the symptoms of fight-or-flight as signs of a serious heart condition since the major symptoms of heart disease are breathlessness, chest pain, as well as palpitations and fainting. However, actual heart disease symptoms are brought on by physical exertion – for example, the harder you exercise, the worse the symptoms become; and symptoms usually go away fairly quickly with rest. This is very different from the fight-or-flight response, which often occurs when you are not exercising or exerting yourself physically. Although the fight-or-flight response can intensify with exercise, this is different from the symptoms of heart disease or a heart attack because fight-or-flight symptoms occur equally often at rest.

Even more importantly, heart disease is very easily detected by physicians. It produces a remarkable electrical signal in the heart which is revealed by an electrocardiogram (EKG). In the fight-or-flight response, the only change that shows up on an EKG is an increase in heart rate (sometimes called tachycardia). By itself, tachycardia is not a sign of danger; unless it reaches an extremely high rate such as over 180 beats per minute, which far exceeds the rates that occur during the fight-or-flight response (120–130 beats per minute). Vigorous physical exercise increases your heart rate to around 150–180 beats per minute. Your usual heart rate when resting is anywhere from 60 to 80 beats per minute, but this varies from person to person.

Another belief is that "too much" of the fight-or-flight response will weaken the heart and make the person more vulnerable to heart attacks or other dangerous physical conditions in the future. Although there is evidence that long lasting stress increases the risk of cardiovascular or cerebral diseases as we get older, chronic stress and strain is very different from the fight-or-light response. As you know by now, fight-or-flight involves short bursts of adrenalin, similar in many ways to what happens during physical exercise. And, of course, we know that exercise-related exertion is very healthy for the body. Although chronically high levels of stress can pose a long-term threat, this risk is minimal compared

From: J. S. Abramowitz & A. E. Braddock: *Hypochondriasis and Health Anxiety*   © 2011 Hogrefe Publishing

to the risks associated with poor lifestyle factors such as a poor diet, lack of exercise, smoking, and substance abuse.

Fainting

The fear of fainting is usually based on the mistaken belief that symptoms such as dizziness and light-headedness mean that one is about to faint. However, the person fails to consider that fight-or-flight arousal is incompatible with fainting. That is, the physical tension (sympathetic nervous system activation) that occurs during fight-or-flight is the exact *opposite* of what happens during fainting spells. Fainting is most likely to occur in people who have low blood pressure, or who respond to stress with major *reductions* in blood pressure. As we know, the fight-or-flight response *increases* heart rate and blood pressure. This is why fainting is extremely rare during fight-or-flight. Another important point is that the fight-or-flight response is designed to *protect* you from harm, so it would make absolutely no sense for nature to develop a response to threat that leads to fainting (which would surely spell the death of the person). Finally, even if you were to faint, consciousness is usually regained within a few seconds. Fainting is simply a way for the body to return to a normal level of functioning.

From: J. S. Abramowitz & A. E. Braddock: *Hypochondriasis and Health Anxiety*   © 2011 Hogrefe Publishing

Body Symptom Handout

My body symptoms:	My threatening thoughts:

From: J. S. Abramowitz & A. E. Braddock: *Hypochondriasis and Health Anxiety*   © 2011 Hogrefe Publishing

Common Thinking Patterns in Health Anxiety

1. **All-or-Nothing Thinking:** You look at things in absolute, black-and-white categories, rather than seeing the middle ground. There is no in-between. Any body sensation becomes a sign of a serious health problem. For example, you are either *completely healthy* or *seriously ill,* and *if you do not get to the doctor at the first sign of trouble, it will be too late.* Another example is, *"Detailed tests are the only way to rule out an illness."*

2. **Fortune-Telling:** You make gloom and doom predictions about things that haven't happened yet, as if you are a fortune teller. For example, *"I'm sure I'll find a lump if I check myself", "If I go to the doctor, he/she'll tell me I'm very sick",* or *"My father died at this age, so I will too."*

3. **Negative Interpretations:** You jump to conclusions and interpret unexplained body sensations as a sign of a serious illness or other medical problem. Anything that seems to feel "not quite right" becomes a serious disease. For example, *"This is not a headache, it's a brain tumor"* or *"The pain in my stomach is a serious illness that no doctors can figure out."*

4. **Intolerance of Uncertainty:** You do not feel satisfied unless you have a complete and agreeable (to you) explanation for the cause and nature of your mysterious body sensations and symptoms. Anything less than a full medical explanation is unacceptable.

5. **Assumptions about**
    Probability: You take it for granted and overestimate the likelihood of catastrophic outcomes – you assume that a generally unlikely event is much more likely to occur than it really is. For example, the idea that serious illnesses and diseases are very easy to catch and lurking everywhere; that you are more vulnerable than others to a certain illness (perhaps because of family history); or the assumption that because you didn't mention something to the doctor, he or she overlooked the presence of a serious health problem.
    Severity: You overestimate the "awfulness" of feared outcomes and automatically assume that negative events, such as having an illness or dying, would be 101% terrible and certainly more horrific or awful than you could cope with. For example, *"I must look after my health at all times, or I will be a terrible burden on my family,"* and *"Death will be lonely and painful (accompanied by images of oneself being self-aware, buried, and eaten by worms)."*

6. **Disqualifying:** You focus only on certain information or facts (usually information that supports your view) but ignore or explain away other facts that are just as relevant (but that do not support your view).

7. **Lofty Standards:** You hold extremely high expectations of others – namely medical professionals – to be able to understand your body symptoms and give you a definitive explanation or cause for everything you think might be wrong with you. This leads to doctor-shopping and continuing to seek out "the best" doctors to explain the unexplainable, or prevent a serious disease.

8. **Intolerance of Anxiety:** You feel that anxiety or discomfort will persist forever unless you do something to escape. Sometimes the fear is that the anxiety or emotional discomfort will spiral out of control or lead to "going crazy," "losing control," or other harmful medical or physical consequences.

From: J. S. Abramowitz & A. E. Braddock: *Hypochondriasis and Health Anxiety*   © 2011 Hogrefe Publishing

Helpful Comments

Responding to requests for reassurance:

- It sounds like you are looking for reassurance about that, but remember we agreed it is not helpful for me to answer those kinds of questions.

- Remember that your urge to get reassurance will go down, but only if I don't answer reassurance questions.

- Remember, the anxiety is temporary. It will go down if you give it time.

- Let's go for a little walk and maybe that will help.

- I know it's hard to resist seeking reassurance. What can I do to help you get through this rough time?

- I've tried to do the right thing, but to avoid an argument, I'll tell you what you want to hear. Still, I don't think you're making a good choice here, but I realize it's hard for you. Make sure you discuss this with your therapist. There will be other chances for you to resist reassurance-seeking.

When the patient succeeds in NOT asking for assurance:

- You're doing a great job not asking for reassurance. I'm proud of you.

- I've noticed the last few days that you've stopped asking questions about your health. I bet that's been difficult for you. Great job.

Exposure Hierarchy Form

Exposure Item	SUDS	Order
1.		
2.		
3.		
4.		
5.		
6.		
7.		
8.		
9.		
10.		
11.		
12.		

From: J. S. Abramowitz & A. E. Braddock: *Hypochondriasis and Health Anxiety*   © 2011 Hogrefe Publishing

10 Tips for Successful Exposure

1. **Exposure practices should be planned, structured, and predictable.** Decide in advance what you will do in the situation and how long you will stay. Plan in advance when you will complete your practice and put it in your schedule. Have a back-up plan in case the original does not work out.

2. **Exposure practices should be repeated frequently.** The more closely spaced the practices, the more fear reduction that you are likely to experience. It is a good idea to practice being in the same situation repeatedly until it becomes easier.

3. **Exposure pace can be gradual.** Do not assume that you must do the most difficult thing you can imagine right away, but be sure to choose practices that are challenging. The more difficult the items that you practice, the quicker you will learn to be more comfortable. Try to choose practices that are challenging but not so difficult that you will not complete them.

4. **Expect to feel uncomfortable.** It is perfectly normal to feel awful during initial exposure practices. Also, these practices may leave you feeling tired and anxious afterwards. With repeated practices, these feelings will decrease. Success should not be judged by how you felt in the situation. Rather, success should be judged by whether you were able to stay in the situation despite feeling awful.

5. **Try not to fight your fear.** Fighting the anxiety will have the effect of increasing your anxious feelings. Instead, just let it happen. The worst thing that is likely to happen is that you will feel temporarily uncomfortable.

6. **Do not use subtle avoidance strategies during exposure.** Complete the practices without the use of distraction, medications, alcohol, asking for reassurance, checking, leaving early, and other such escape strategies.

7. **Use exposure practices to test negative predictions about the consequences of facing your fear.** Before beginning an exposure, ask yourself what you are afraid might happen during the practice. Then conduct the exposure practice to test the accuracy of your fearful prediction. Afterwards, think about the evidence you gained from your experience and how it compares to your original fearful prediction.

8. **Rate your fear on scale from 0 to 100.** During exposure practices it can be helpful to pay attention to how you are feeling and to notice the variables that make your anxiety go up and down during the practice.

9. **Exposure practices should last long enough for a significant reduction in anxiety.** Continue each exposure practice until your anxiety goes down, no matter how much time it takes. A good rule of thumb is to continue an exposure practice until your anxiety rating on the 0–100 scale decreases by at least half (e.g., below 40 if it peaked at 80).

10. **If possible, practice in a variety of settings.** Conducting exposure practices in multiple settings will help bring about a more broad decrease in your anxiety. It is often helpful to conduct exposures with your therapist, at home, and in other settings. It can also be helpful to conduct some exposures by yourself because sometimes the presence of other people can make us feel artificially safe.

From: J. S. Abramowitz & A. E. Braddock: *Hypochondriasis and Health Anxiety*   © 2011 Hogrefe Publishing

Exposure Practice Form

Name:_____ Date: _____ Time: _____ Session #: ____

1. Description of the exposure practice:

2. Every 5 minutes during the exposure, rate SUDS from 0 to 100:

3. SUDS when beginning exposure (0–100) _____

SUDS	SUDS	SUDS	SUDS	SUDS
1._____	7._____	13._____	19._____	25._____
2._____	8._____	14._____	20._____	26._____
3._____	9._____	15._____	21._____	27._____
4._____	10._____	16._____	22._____	28._____
5._____	11._____	17._____	23._____	29._____
6._____	12._____	18._____	24._____	30._____

7. Comments:

Help with Response Prevention

- Specific response prevention instructions:

- *Choose* not to engage in safety behaviors.
- If you are having trouble choosing to resist:
  - Remember that the urge is based on a mistaken belief or assumption. You don't *really* need to do *that* to feel better or reduce the chances of being ill.
  - Find someone to talk to and ask them to stay with you until the urge passes.
  - Leave the situation for a while (if possible) to get away from reminders.
  - **If you perform a safety behavior**, immediately record it on a self-monitoring form and discuss it with your therapist. Then, deliberately re-expose yourself to the situation that evoked the safety behavior.

From: J. S. Abramowitz & A. E. Braddock: *Hypochondriasis and Health Anxiety*   © 2011 Hogrefe Publishing

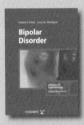

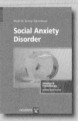
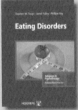
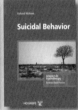

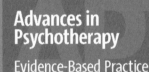